The ULTIMATE PONZI

The ULTIMATE PONZI

The Scott Rothstein Story

By Chuck Malkus

PELICAN PUBLISHING COMPANY

Gretna 2013

The word "Pelican" and the depiction of a pelican are
trademarks of Pelican Publishing Company, Inc., and are
registered in the U.S. Patent and Trademark Office.

Library of Congress Cataloging-in-Publication Data

Malkus, Chuck.
   The ultimate Ponzi : the Scott Rothstein story / by Chuck Malkus.
      p. cm.
      ISBN 978-1-4556-1786-9 (hbk. : alk. paper) — ISBN 978-1-
4556-1787-6 (e-book) 1. Rothstein, Scott, 1962- 2. Swindlers and
swindling—United States—Biography. 3. Ponzi schemes—United
States—Case studies. 4. Fraud—United States—Case studies. I.
Title.
   HV6692.R68M35 2013
   364.16'3092—dc23
                                                        2012036717

Front-jacket photograph: From The Miami Herald, June 21, 2007
©2007 The Miami Herald. All rights reserved. Used by permission.

Printed in the United States of America
Published by Pelican Publishing Company, Inc.
1000 Burmaster Street, Gretna, Louisiana 70053

Contents

Acknowledgments

The major difference between Scott Rothstein and Bernie Madoff is that from the outset, Rothstein not only seemed a comic book caricature but also infiltrated the entire Fort Lauderdale community. Madoff, on the other hand, kept a low profile and was relatively unknown until his arrest. As a result, there were a number of people with whom I corresponded in order to track down the most up-to-date and insightful information.

One of the first challenges in writing this book was to find people in the tri-county area of Miami-Dade, Broward, and Palm Beach counties who were willing to be interviewed when there was a tremendous amount of information in the news about Rothstein and his ties to mobsters, crooked sheriff's deputies, corrupt politicians, and overall villains. In the beginning, I was encouraged by former law enforcement officials to abort this journalistic mission and instead write the story as a fiction book.

I quickly learned that there were several reasons to proceed with documenting Scott Rothstein's story—he had not only taken advantage of charitable organizations and given a black eye to an entire community, but also he had impacted hundreds of lives. I felt that this scoundrel had hurt so many people that his story must be told and that, in the end, even the mafia organizations would gain an appreciation of where this guy had come from and how he did what he did.

In the beginning, I publicly announced myself as the author

of the Scott Rothstein Book at a number of civic breakfasts and luncheons. I wanted to let those with whom I had worked over the past two decades know that I was writing this project and that I'd be interested in speaking with them. Given the sensitivity of the ongoing criminal investigations and sometimes the fear that perhaps one day Rothstein would be set free, many of the people interviewed did so only on the condition that their names would not be used. As time passed, many honorable citizens stepped forward and spoke about their experiences.

I was fortunate to surround myself with a team of professionals who have helped dig and get the facts, beginning with my private editor, Chauncey Mabe. I am grateful to Chauncey for going the extra mile with research, valuable insight, and continual updates over the span of two years. I also appreciate the efforts and guidance of my two Pelican Publishing editors, Nina Kooij and Abi Pollokoff.

This book could not have been completed without the help of a number of hard-working attorneys and reputable law firms, which include, in no particular order, Richard Zaden of Seiler, Sautter, Zaden, Rimes, & Weihe; Jeff Cutler of De La Cruz & Cutler; Mark Booth of Rogers, Morris, & Ziegler; Blosser & Sayfie; Phillips Eisinger & Koss; Anthony Russo and Harry Cohen of the Russo Law Firm; Michael Freedland; Daniel Gass; and Bradley Cohen. Of course, there were many more attorneys who shared information off the record and I appreciate all of their insights.

I wish to offer a special thanks to professionals at the accounting firm of Marcum LLP, especially to Larry H. Blum, and to the team of accountants at Accounting, Tax & Business Solutions. I am also indebted to the forensic accountants at MRW Consulting Group, including Ronald E. Wise, Luis O. Rivera, and Jose Marrero. It took several accountants and a gargantuan effort to begin to piece together the enormous Rothstein puzzle.

I'd also like to thank two psychologists for sharing how a man like Scott Rothstein could be so manipulative and destructive. Dr. Joan Pastor of Beverly Hills, California, and Dr. Stephen Greenspan of the University of Colorado provided information that helped me place things in the proper perspective.

David Welch and James King at Universal Court Reporting helped me to stay focused on the bigger picture with this project. To the many friends and associates who offered countless encouragement throughout the long investigative process—too many people to recognize by name—I'd like to say thank you once again.

There are several reporters from newspapers, television stations, and magazines who have provided information and source material. In no particular order, they include the following people.

One of the hardest-working journalists covering the Rothstein story was Bob Norman, first at *New Times* and then as a television reporter with the ABC affiliate WPLG Local 10. I also salute the teams of journalists at the *South Florida Sun Sentinel* and the *South Florida Business Journal.* Reporters with the *Miami Herald, Daily Business Review, Wall Street Journal, New York Times, Palm Beach Post, Associated Press, Reuters, Businessweek,* WFOR-TV, WTVJ, WSVN, CNN, and a number of others.

I enjoyed sharing part of this story on the CNBC *American Greed* documentary under executive producer Charles Schaeffer and with my friend Aphrodite Jones, who provided a stellar documentary on *Investigative Discovery.* Another source of reason on the Rothstein spectacle was *Gold Coast Magazine* publisher Bernie McCormick. I feel that it is also important to mention that *Sun Sentinel* publisher Howard Greenberg is doing South Florida a big favor by continuing to commit staff to covering this story during the months and years ahead.

I couldn't have persevered through this roller coaster of a story without the fantastic support of my wife and researcher, Sandra Padilla Malkus. There are not too many wives who would allow their husbands to spend hours tracking down seedy individuals, including exotic dancers, escorts, and corrupt law enforcement officers. Finally, I could not have completed this project without my parents. One of my best line editors was my do-it-all mom, Conaere Rose Malkus, who always believed in the importance of telling the truth, while my dad, Chuck Malkus III, has supported my efforts to make a difference and meet new challenges since I was a boy.

Introduction

The first major South Florida charity event for the fall of 2009 came two days before Halloween at the multi-million dollar mansion of Fort Lauderdale attorney Scott Rothstein and his petite blonde wife, Kim. Ordinarily, I avoided Rothstein, a vulgar arriviste who had bought his way into Fort Lauderdale society with lavish donations to charities and hospitals. But the timing of this soirée seemed too good to pass up. After years of whispered speculation of where Rothstein's money had come from, terrifying gossip had started to emanate from the Bank of America Tower on Las Olas Boulevard, where his upstart law firm, Rothstein Rosenfeldt Adler, had its headquarters. Some kind of implosion appeared imminent. I didn't want to miss a thing that might happen at the Rothstein waterfront home that night in tiny Harbor Beach, one of Fort Lauderdale's most elite neighborhoods.

As guests arrived, we were given a show of a few of the cars from Scottie's collection, including a Bugatti, a Maserati, and a Ferrari. There were $4 million worth of automobiles sitting in the driveway. Upon entering the home, we were presented with a glass of champagne. Lovely, white-gloved servers circulated trays of hors d'oeuvres. Many of the guests, employees of nonprofit charities, earned less in one year than the cost of the evening's party. Few of the 150 people in attendance had been to a $6 million mansion before, let alone stood next to a mega-yacht. Yet, right there at the dock

11

out back sat Rothstein's eighty-seven-foot pleasure boat, the Princess Kimberly. Like me, these underpaid toilers in the fields of good works were there, despite the ostensible reason for the occasion, to gawk at their host—sure to be dressed in one of his $8,000 Italian suits—and his riches. After all, this was the lawyer who had donated more than $6 million to one cause or another over the preceding two years, a lawyer of whom, a mere six years before, no one in Fort Lauderdale had ever heard. We wanted to see how Scottie was bearing up under the increasing pressure.

As the evening wore on, however, and there was no sign of Rothstein, rumors and remarks burbled through the crowd. After the first hour, I overheard a man who had already enjoyed a couple of glasses of champagne say, "I saw Scott Rothstein about forty minutes ago. He had a bottle and he was headed upstairs."

As we ate his food, drank his booze, and mocked his taste in, well, everything, Scott Rothstein jokes punctuated the rest of the evening, spoken just out of the hearing of Kimmie, who soldiered on with a stiff spine and a determined expression, dressed in an ensemble that easily could have bought a month's groceries for a family of four—not including the jewelry, which could have financed a middle-class dwelling. Kim, a former bartender, married to Rothstein slightly more than a year, supplied some gracious welcoming remarks. In Scott's absence, it fell to his partner Stuart Rosenfeldt to give a speech.

"I was hoping to see Scott there," Rosenfeldt later told me. "A lot of people were looking for him that night. Something funky was going on. I didn't know what it was, but it was unusual for him to miss this event."

No kidding, Stuart.

If Rosenfeldt thought that night was unusual, it's only because he had no idea what was about to befall him.

On Friday, the day following the party, Stuart returned

to his office after lunch to find a stack of phone messages waiting for him. Each one was from a friend of Rothstein. There were five messages from hedge-fund maven George Levin alone. "Certain people I know to be friends of Scott called me and said, 'We can't find Scott,'" Rosenfeldt recalled. Each one of these friends of Scott was also an investor in his elaborate sideline of pre-trial settlement products, and they were clamoring for their money. Regularly scheduled payments were due and overdue. They figured Rosenfeldt had access to their cash. "No one can do that," Stuart said to one after the other. No one, it turned out, could access Scott's investment accounts, held separately from the firm's legal business, except for Scott. Certainly not Stuart, who insisted throughout the prolonged legal hell that followed that he managed only the firm's legitimate legal business.

Quickly enough, over a heady few days in late October and early November 2009, Fort Lauderdale and the rest of the country began to learn the outlines of a stupendous scandal involving the community's top philanthropist, an employment lawyer who had come seemingly out of nowhere to build Fort Lauderdale's richest law firm. At last, we knew how he did it—Scott was a con artist, plundering investor accounts and concocting the biggest Ponzi scheme in Florida history in order to build RRA and fund his own extravagant lifestyle. Even for the many insiders in the local legal community, those who knew that Scott was spending more money than it was possible to earn in the practice of law, the news came as a shock. Everyone had thought his riches had come from money laundering or Internet porn.

Now he had fled, leaving less than $200,000 in RRA's accounts—barely enough to cover payroll for the firm's clerical employees and administrative staff. It looked as though Scott had gotten away clean, flying to Morocco on a chartered jet after having his own staff attorneys research the question of which countries have no extradition treaties with either the United States or Israel. With $18 million—$200 million, by other accounts—he could live comfortably with a bodyguard or two in relative safety. American law could not touch him.

The story of greed, corruption, and sex, involving Israeli mobsters, wealthy car dealers, escort services, gentlemen's clubs, forged judges' signatures, charities, socialites, national politicians, murder, and suicide and the unraveling of the biggest Ponzi scheme in Florida history, totaled at $1.4 billion, would proceed without him. Before it was over, more than his partners and associates at RRA would be tainted— so would judges, cops, religious leaders, and businessmen. Money really does change everything, especially if the denominations are big enough.

And then Scott, as he loved to do, astonished everyone. He flew home to face the music.

The ULTIMATE PONZI

Chapter 1

Origin of a Player

By all accounts, Scott Rothstein is the product of a normal upbringing by loving, working-class parents. No evidence exists to suggest that he was a bad seed, evil, or without conscience from birth, and he certainly is no classic sociopath like those who tear the wings off insects or torture animals as children. On the contrary, credible testimony from people who knew him as a child, a teenager, and a young lawyer presents a picture of a well-mannered son who made friends easily even though he was a bit shy. From a Jewish family, the young Scott was religious, a trait that carried over into his adulthood and further into his years of con artistry, and it is doubtless that it helped fool some of the investors who later became his victims. It certainly influenced his partner, Stuart Rosenfeldt, a Protestant convert who admired Scott's dedication to his Jewish faith. And, indeed, that faith appears to have been sincere—he was a hypocrite, perhaps, but not a cynic. He also had a beautiful singing voice, a talent recognized by the cantor at his temple and also by his teachers at Boyd Anderson High School, where he was one of the leaders of the chorus, his primary extracurricular activity. Mark Booth, a Fort Lauderdale lawyer who attended Nova Southeastern Law School with Scott, remarked, "You know, it's almost like Scott tried to make up for being in the school choir."

Scott Rothstein in front of a wall of photos in his office at Rothstein Rosenfeldt Adler. (Courtesy *Daily Business Review*)

Scott Rothstein was born on June 10, 1962, in the Bronx. The theatrical flair that made him a successful competitor in the chorus and doubtlessly served him well as a fraudster comes from his mother, Gay. As a young woman, she briefly attended the famous High School of Performing Arts in New York, the so-called *Fame* school, but she was kicked out for a succession of minor infractions, the last being gum-chewing in ballet class. Both parents worked hard to provide for Scott and his sister, Ronni. Harvey Rothstein, Scott's father, was a sales representative for condom manufacturers for thirty-seven years (a fact held up to ridicule on blog sites after Scott's disgrace), while Gay held a variety of jobs in New York, including stints in the garment district, at a toy company, and at a Hebrew day school. Scott may have had a mobbed-up uncle, who gave him a glimpse of a darker yet more glamorous side of life. Gary Phillips, a lawyer Scott worked for in the late 1990s, recalled how Scott used to talk about an uncle with "certain connections" and bragged about going up on a roof in the Bronx to watch his uncle beat people up, presumably for failing to pay loan shark or gambling debts. If this story is true, then the influence of this shadowy uncle could account for Scott's penchant for dressing and talking like "a Brooklyn-type tough guy," which began to surface as early as law school, according to Nova classmates.

While Scott's parents have mostly shied away from the press and declined my repeated requests for an interview, they did present a compelling portrait of their son's upbringing in the so-called "leniency letter" written for the benefit of Judge James I. Cohn of the US District Court in the sentencing phase of Scott's 2010 trial. True, Gay and Harvey were hoping to present a favorable impression of Scott as a person with redeeming qualities who might be able to make a contribution to society should Cohn see fit to let him out of prison before the end of his natural life. And yet the Rothsteins' letter strikes me as sincere and reliable as to the facts of Scott's early life in "a lower-middle-class family who never had the wherewithal to give him many of the things that came easily to the families of his friends." When they add that theirs was a caring and loving family, I believe them.

The parents write that Scott was a good student and identified as "intellectually gifted" by his schools in New York. He was, and I put these words down with no irony intended, a Boy Scout who attended Hebrew school, though without much joy or dedication. His parents said that "he was sweet and lovable and just mischievous enough to keep us on our toes." Scott's parents portray the boy as a good brother to his sister, three years younger, though the relationship was not without its "rivalries and battles." In the Bronx, Scott's family lived across the hall from his grandparents, and he grew especially close to "Grams," who, at the writing of the leniency letter in June 2010, was still alive at the age of ninety-nine. The cantor at the Reform temple where young Scott studied for his bar mitzvah first noticed Scott's musical talent and encouraged him to sing in the choir. "This experience gave him two of the things he loved: Judaism and music. The older he got, the more important both those things became."

No evidence suggests that Scott's mother and father were anything but loving, devoted parents, and he returned that devotion to the very end. Indeed, some observers in Fort Lauderdale most familiar with the case suspect that he returned from Morocco only because mobsters defrauded in the Ponzi scheme would have threatened his parents, and possibly his wife, if he did not. A glimpse of Scott's feelings for his parents can be found in his own mitigation letter to Judge Cohn. He wrote about his parents' financial struggles—"The only fights I remember my parents having were about money"—but added that "money was never an end-all for any of us. What my parents and grandparents lacked in financial resources they more than made up for with love, caring, and compassion." His next words seemed almost laughable, given the greed and vulgarity of his life as a Ponzi tycoon: "My parents and grandparents taught my sister and me the importance of family, respect for others, and the importance of honesty, education, and hard work, and moreover, the mantra of giving back. We were taught that as little as we had, there were always those less fortunate. And we gave of our time and money, even it meant going without." Like his parents in their letter, Scott was obviously attempting to influence Judge Cohn with a show of contrition and family values, but the family feeling he expressed has a genuine ring to it, and I believe that for a substantial period in his early life, he had not yet become obsessed with money and the power and luxury it could bring.

Gay and Harvey moved the family to South Florida in 1976, when Scott was fourteen. He enrolled as a freshman

Scott Rothstein in his Harbor Beach home.

at Boyd Anderson High School, where he sang in the chorus, the Chamber Singers, and the Barbershop Quartet, all under the tutelage of music teacher James Long. The parents quoted a letter from Long: "My memories of Scott will always be of that incredibly talented, dedicated, and generous young man-musician whom I had the pleasure to know and work with at Boyd Anderson." I can't help imagining this was followed by, "What happened to turn him into a monster?" but if so, Gay and Harvey did not share it with the court, although everyone present must certainly have harbored the thought. How did this sweet, generous, musical boy become the greatest white-collar criminal in Florida history, fleecing and betraying his closest friends? Pat Straw Cavenaugh, who works as a law secretary for Mark Booth, went to high school with Scott and sang with him in the elite Chamber Singers. "He was very good," she recalled. "We toured around the county and did state competitions. I was shocked when all this [scandal] happened with him. I was just amazed that he could have done this. I didn't think it was the Scott Rothstein I went to school with. But then I got out my yearbook and it all came together."

Scott had plenty of friends, according to Gay and Harvey, which is certainly believable given the charm and salesmanship later on display during his run as the most flamboyant lawyer in South Florida. "The mark of any good con man is the ability to get people to like them," former State Senator Steve Geller, a Broward County Commission candidate, told reporters in the immediate aftermath of Scott's disgrace. "The guy certainly spoke a great game." Among Scott's high school friends was Debbie Safra, who later became the mother of Scott's only child, a daughter born out of wedlock shortly before his first marriage to another local lawyer, Kimberly Hill, in 1993. In high school, Scott and Debbie were nothing more than friends in the same circle; their brief romance blossomed after his graduation from law school in 1988. Gay and Harvey wrote that Scott chose law over music so he could make a living, another endeavor for which he seemed to have an inborn talent. "He was brilliant in the courtroom," people said.

Scott's legal talent proved to be real, and it was first noticed during his time at Nova Southeastern Law School. Booth, who was one year behind Rothstein, remembers a striking example of Scott's legal skill. It came during the Upper Class competition. "I thought Scott was going to be murdered in the finals," Booth recalled. In the halls of the school, he said, Scott behaved like a macho tough guy—an early version of the mafia persona Scott later cultivated at Rothstein Rosenfeldt Adler—not the kind of person possessing the legal mind or rhetorical skills needed to do well in court. "Man, was I wrong," said Booth. "I was really impressed with how he handled himself in front of the judges in the competition. I realized his everyday persona was just an act. When he got in front of the podium and started his presentation and when he got hit with the questions, he acted lawyer-like. He came across as a totally professional lawyer."

Scott worked his way through law school, in part with a job at a Braman car dealership. Stuart Rosenfeldt recalled: "At a John McCain fundraiser held at his house, Scott came downstairs with his employee ID from when he worked for Norman Braman when he was still in college. He showed it to Norman Braman and talked about how he worked in 'F & I' closing car deals." By 2008, he had come a long way.

After graduating from Nova Southeastern Law School, Scott first went to work at the law firm of Gunther & Whitaker, where a lawyer named Robert H. Schwartz became, in Scott's later assessment, his mentor. "As I remember," said Schwartz, "he started working for us [as a clerk] when he was a law student at Nova. There were eleven lawyers in those days and he worked for all of us." Scott pitched in to help with insurance defense cases as well as general civil practice. "I trusted him to always do a good job," Schwartz said. "He worked for us for two or three years before moving on." When the Ponzi-scheme story broke twenty-five years later, Schwartz was shocked: "I would have never thought Scott could do something that was dishonest."

Leaving Gunther & Whitaker, Scott briefly set up a one-man shop in Plantation, a Fort Lauderdale suburb, as a lawyer specializing in "routine" labor and employment cases. In 1991 he formed a partnership, Kusnick & Rothstein, with Howard Kusnick, who later played a significant role in some of the legal and financial shenanigans at RRA and eventually was sentenced to two years in prison for his participation. During this period, Scott made a decent living practicing law, according to a November 9, 2009, story in the *Miami Herald,* but he wasn't getting rich by any stretch of the imagination. In 1993, he married Kim Hill. One break for Scott came in 1998, when he signed on to represent the Plantation police union in discipline disputes. By all accounts, he was a hard-working and competent lawyer—perhaps more than competent. The *Miami Herald* reported on December 7, 2009, "when he was at the table, he was as good as it gets," said Michael Hanlon, president of the Plantation chapter of the Fraternal Order of Police. "Scott was a very well-informed and very skillful negotiator."

I believe the evidence suggests that it was during this period, the late 1990s, that Scott's moral compass began to go haywire, probably in a gradual and incremental process. A very bright man with talent and charisma, he may have started to see himself as a child of destiny, intended for grander things. Kim Hill worked for a large firm, and I think watching his wife interact with her bosses led Scott to conceive the notion that at a large practice the leading partners don't have to work very hard. They serve instead as figureheads, facilitators—the public face of the company raking in the larger part of the firm's income, which of course is exactly how he ran RRA in 2005 (with the addition of a Ponzi scheme to bankroll his dreams of power and influence as well as an extravagant lifestyle). Many people in retrospect have commented about how Scott practiced so little law at RRA that it almost seemed like he didn't like being a lawyer, only the perks and power that came with being a partner in a big, important firm. But as we've seen, in his early career, Scott is remembered as a talented practitioner.

Another factor leading Scott off the rails may be found in the mitigation letter he wrote to Judge Cohn:

> Looking back, however, lurking just below the surface was a person so fearful of failure and so terrified of ever having to struggle the way his parents did, that it translated into an acute anxiety disorder that was, at times, debilitating, and for which I continue to seek treatment today. Moreover, I realize that it translated into an underlying set of character defects and personality flaws that would ultimately never allow me to accept any type of failure on my part. These traits would lay dormant for many years, held in check by countervailing principles that were the foundation of my family upbringing, until my ego allowed them to manifest themselves in the form of an individual so narcissistic that I would do anything to avoid any type of chink in my armor; anything that would make me look less than uber-successful and perfect in every detail.

This is dime-store self-analysis, of course, intended to inspire pity in the judge's heart, but I detect at least a grain of truth in it. Fear of failure, a return to childhood penury, and the anxiety of perfectionism are as good an explanation as any for Scott's warped character and criminal behavior. Could such childish traits cause Scott to become a thief and a liar, with respect for no person and no principle, including the law itself? Yes, I think it is possible. As Scott also wrote in the letter to Judge Cohn, the financial pressures on his family did not relent until he had been a lawyer for seven years and finally reached the point where he was earning enough money "to help ease the financial burden" for his parents and sister. In any event, at some point Scott began to cut corners, lie, and cheat clients, long before he founded RRA and began the infamous Ponzi scheme.

In one early sign of things to come, Scott angered police officers in Fort Lauderdale when he filed an age discrimination suit against the Fraternal Order of Police and the city. This was when he represented the Plantation FOP in labor and other disputes with the city. While he managed to retain the loyalty and friendship of Plantation cops—he hired more than one as bodyguards during his RRA glory days—their Fort Lauderdale counterparts felt that he took the case against their union out of "ego and greed," as Jack Lokeinsky, Fort Lauderdale FOP president, told me. To make matters worse, Rothstein's side did not prevail in the case.

Scott's next big break came in 2000, when he was invited to join a medium-sized and thriving firm in Hollywood, Florida, Phillips Eisinger Koss & Rosenfeldt, as a name partner. By then, some of the traits that later blossomed into flamboyant extravagance and led to his downfall were already beginning to be visible. "When he joined us he had two Porsches and a Harley," recalled managing partner Gary D. Phillips. "I said, 'Scott, Kim must make a ton of money.' He said no, they owned a couple of apartment buildings. At the time we let him go he was driving a Ferrari. I don't know how he could afford it and couldn't figure out what he was doing." This, however, is hindsight. For a long time, Phillips liked and trusted Rothstein. "Scott was a master at getting close to people and getting them to trust him," Phillips said. "If he had used his force for good instead of evil, he could have been Luke Skywalker instead of Darth Vader. He just wasn't willing to put forth the work."

Phillips hired Rothstein at the suggestion of Stuart Rosenfeldt. The practice needed a labor and employment attorney, recalled Phillips, and Rosenfeldt spoke highly of his friend Scott Rothstein. The two men, Rosenfeldt and Rothstein, first met in the early 1990s during a legal convention at the Broward County Convention Center, when Rosenfeldt came away with a distinctively negative impression: "I didn't like him. He had an arrogant side," Rosenfeldt told me in August 2010. "Cocky I think is the best word. Just better than anyone else. I wish I had stayed with my instincts." Instead, the two men gradually became friends. First, Rosenfeldt recalled, they had a case against each other, which they resolved without trial, and then they competed for a client, with neither landing the business. Finally, the two lawyers attended a seminar at St. Petersburg, where they got to know each other better, and they started talking every Saturday, when each would go to the office to catch up on the week's workload. "It was a positive relationship at first," Rosenfeldt reflected. "Scott was always encouraging me. Scott built me up. Scott was always cheerful and everybody liked him."

When Rosenfeldt found out that his friend was negotiating to join another firm, Becker & Poliakoff, he persuaded Phillips to offer Rosenfeldt a job. "As a lawyer Scott had incredible self confidence and speaking skills," Rosenfeldt said. "He had charisma. He was a great trial lawyer. He had an eye for money and an eye for making money and an eye to recruit good clients."

At first, Phillips had no reason to disagree. Scott brought with him Debra Villegas, his clerk, when he joined the firm, and later hired his protégée Melissa Britt Lewis when she graduated law school, but he displayed little of the flamboyance that later characterized his time as downtown

Fort Lauderdale's most prominent attorney. "We did have a 'no jeans' policy and Scott would break it," Phillips recalled. "He said they were expensive jeans." Phillips began to sour on Rothstein when he learned that Scott's wife, Kimberly Ann Hill, did not know about his illegitimate daughter, by then eight or nine years old. But these were matters of personal character. Things didn't go seriously wrong for Scott in terms of his professional relationship with Phillips until about two years later. "Scott believed in growth," Phillips said, describing the strategy Rothstein employed without restraint at RRA. "He believed if you hire people then the firm will have leverage and growth. But he was hiring people we didn't have work for. Scott just wanted to hire and hire." The labor and employment department under Scott had grown to eight attorneys and accounted for twenty percent of the firm's revenue. Unfortunately, it also accounted for forty percent of the expenses. "We were losing twenty percent of our revenue to keep this practice alive," Phillips said. "We had to let go the bulk of the attorneys in this practice group."

What's more, in another development presaging Rothstein's reign at RRA, he no longer seemed to practice much law. "He wasn't getting legal work done in a timely manner," Phillips said. "Clients would call and we'd have to designate someone else to get the work done. He used to tell me where his wife worked her firm had eighty lawyers across the state. The top guys were making $2 million a year without working hard."

Despite all of this, Phillips found he could not help from liking Scott. "He had that personality," he said. "Very few people have that type of strong charisma." For a time, the two men were close—Phillips and his wife celebrated his forty-fifth birthday with Scott and his wife. For two years, Phillips had lunch with Scott two or three times a week. "I thought I knew the man, and at the time I thought we had common interests and goals," Phillips said. "Because of that, we gave him tremendous leeway on hiring and developing his department. I thought I knew him pretty well. Obviously, I didn't. I only knew what he wanted me to know of him." Among the things Scott wanted Phillips to know was that he was a religious man of high moral fiber. For example, he told Phillips he "wrapped tefillin" each morning. In the Jewish tradition, tefillin—tiny leather boxes, also known as phylacteries, containing written prayers—are attached with leather straps to the arms and forehead, a ritual accompanied by the recitation of prayers. The idea is that a man who wraps, or in a more common parlance, lays, tefillin is devout and disciplined. "That's how he said he would start his day," Phillips said. "He told me he was active in Jewish causes and with his synagogue. I don't know if any of it is true."

After Scott left the firm, taking Stuart Rosenfeldt with him to downtown Fort Lauderdale to start what would become RRA, Phillips heard rumors that Rothstein had been engaged in an affair with one of the associates. "One of the other associates saw the two of them together in the garage," he says. "It was said one of the associates got better treatment because she was having an affair with Scott." These kind of rumors trailed Scott everywhere he worked, even after he made himself rich at RRA and started availing himself of strippers, escorts, and other such women.

Phillips remained unaware of any of this while Scott was working at his firm. There were other things he didn't know about, too. One was a secret campaign to cause conflict between Phillips and Rosenfeldt, or alternately to inspire feelings of discontent in Rosenfeldt so the older attorney would leave and start a new firm with Rothstein. After a brief honeymoon period at Phillips Eisinger, Scott began telling Rosenfeldt that he "shouldn't tolerate" certain actions and statements by Phillips, but should take offense at them instead. Actually, Phillips was usually reacting to "negatives put into play by Scott" on the sly, Rosenfeldt now sees, with the express purpose of causing a rift with Phillips. Rothstein had ambitious plans to open a new practice in downtown Fort Lauderdale, and he needed a seasoned lawyer with a good reputation—like Rosenfeldt—to be his partner.

"That's where Scott wedged me first," Rosenfeldt said. "I feel sorry for Gary Phillips since I hurt him in leaving. I also left a good livelihood. In hindsight, I never should have left. But Scott needed my credentials to give him an air of credibility and now I feel that I was used. I never set out for the money." Still, after a little more than two years at Phillips Eisinger, Scott was able to persuade Rosenfeldt to decamp. "Scott and I made the decision to leave the firm," Rosenfeldt recalled. The plan was that Rothstein would oversee the business aspect of the new firm they would found together and take care of the financial side, while Rosenfeldt, who enjoyed being a lawyer and mentoring young attorneys, would supervise the employment and labor practice at what was envisioned as "Rothstein & Rosenfeldt."

In actuality, it didn't go quite as smoothly as that. Rather than an orderly departure to start a new firm with a new partner, Scott was fired from Phillips Eisinger for ethical lapses that sound especially significant in retrospect: he lied to a client about filing court documents. As Phillips recalls, a client phoned to discuss a complaint and an emergency motion for injunctive relief that Scott was supposedly handling. "I went to look at the file and found there was no file," Phillips said. "He told the client he had already filed these motions. I pushed [the other partners] to get rid of him after that." It fell to Phillips to take up the case and file the motions to cover for Rothstein. He did not report Rothstein to the Florida Bar. He told the *Daily Business Review* on December 15, 2009, concluding the issue "was not grievable." By this point, Rothstein and Rosenfeldt were already well into planning their departure. "I was in trial when Scott called me and said, 'They asked me to leave, but ha ha ha, we're leaving already,'" Rosenfeldt said, adding that he never knew the exact nature of why Scott was booted from Phillips Eisinger.

It's useful to keep this story in mind when trying to determine the arc of Scott Rothstein's descent from an ordinary, hardworking lawyer to a practitioner willing to cut corners and lie to clients to one eager to defraud clients, friends, or anyone who could further his grandiose ambitions. Consider one last story, this from attorney Mark Booth: in late 2006 and early 2007, Booth had a client who had fathered an illegitimate child. The man, a recovering drug addict, hired Booth in an attempt to gain custody from his ex-girlfriend, a drug addict who had violated probation and gone on the lam. He asked Booth about the chance of getting child support from the child's mother. "I said that you should gain custody, but it is very unlikely you will see any support," recalled Booth, who at the time assumed that a fugitive drug addict would have no funds. "He then told me she had access to money." It seemed that Rothstein had represented the mother in a suit against an employer who had fired her during an earlier pregnancy. Scott prevailed, collecting a settlement worth "a considerable amount of money, close to $300,000." The problem was that Rothstein settled the case and received the money without bothering to tell his client, who did not learn of it until several years later.

"My client told me the two of them would go to Rothstein's office, after she had called and threatened to turn him into the bar," Booth said. "Rothstein would hand over fists full of money which they then would go use [for drugs]. When they ran out of money, they would go back and get more."

This went on for some time, until the couple broke up, the man went to rehab, and the woman went underground. In the custody case, Rothstein again represented the woman, even though she was nowhere to be found, assigning the case to a junior attorney. "[The junior attorney's] initial call to me was that this woman is a very good friend of Scott Rothstein," Booth said. "This woman, who was a fugitive, who had violated probation." In the course of the custody battle, Booth came into possession of a court document that he says was evidence that Rothstein had won the discrimination case for his client. Later, in the summer of 2010, when he read Scott's mitigation letter to Judge Cohn, he knew that Rothstein was lying about when he first started to break bad. "I saw the document from the discrimination case in about 2009," Booth says. "It was six months to a year before the [RRA] collapse. The document was about ten years old. It was from the late 1990s or 2000." That means Scott was stealing from clients at least five years earlier than he admits in the mitigation letter to Judge Cohn.

. And what happened to the man seeking child support for his daughter? "We got the child," Booth said. "Custody was no problem. We had a court order stating that [the mother] must pay child support. My client and I decided to let it sit for six months. I was planning to depose [Rothstein] and have him admit that he owed this woman money. And then garnish him. I'd be able to collect money for my client. That was the game plan. When my client read the newspaper [about Rothstein's disgrace], he gave me a call. The rest is history."

A recovered drug addict, trying to get make a new life for himself, denied child support he otherwise would have received—another victim of Scott Rothstein.

Chapter 2

The First Big Seduction

Hardly anyone noticed when Scott Rothstein and Stuart Rosenfeldt opened their new law office in downtown Fort Lauderdale in 2002. A small shop of seven lawyers, the practice specialized in labor and employment law from an address in a spanking new office building located at the corner of Northeast Third Avenue and Northeast Second Street, a block from the more prestigious addresses on Las Olas Boulevard. Although founding partners Rosenfeldt and Rothstein had a plan—or, Rothstein had a plan that he shared in bits and pieces with Rosenfeldt—a couple of years would pass before the practice started drawing the kind of attention that would make it the most glamorous and talked-about law firm in South Florida, if not the entire state.

"Our primary motivation was to get away from Gary Phillips," Rosenfeldt recalled. "Downtown Fort Lauderdale was where the action was. We thought this would be a good place to hang our shingles." The plan, as far as Rosenfeldt was concerned, was for Scott to manage the business side of the firm, while he oversaw and conducted much of the litigation and the other details of actual lawyering. Rothstein, who spoke to his partner of vague investments that had paid off handsomely, was also going to finance the practice and its growth, while Rosenfeldt lent his expertise, his reputation, and his contacts. The partners were supposed to plan and manage everything in close consultation, but it didn't quite work out that way.

Instead, Scott made decisions on his own, principally about hiring lawyers and merging with other firms, informing Stuart only after the fact. Scott simply did not follow the business model of most law firms. In fact, it should be noted that Stuart Rosenfeldt was another Scott Rothstein victim.

Rosenfeldt was an unlikely figure to be caught up in even an indirect association with an international financial scandal. Growing up in Philadelphia, he knew from a young age that he wanted to become a labor and employment lawyer so that he could make a difference for both employers and workers. His father, Joseph, ran a small trucking company, and Rosenfeldt remembered the day he overheard attorneys advising his dad about how to respond to union organizers. "There was a union organizing campaign and I watched the lawyers strategizing in my basement," Rosenfeldt recalled. "And I said, 'That's what I want to do when I grow up.'"

Another event that left a lasting impact on Rosenfeldt came when his mother, Loretta, was diagnosed with multiple sclerosis. He was six. Throughout his childhood, he was admonished not to do or say anything that might cause her stress. "My father said, 'Whatever you do, don't upset your mother. No fighting, no conflicts.' That dictum is what developed my personality over time, looking back. I'm a lawyer, but I do not like conflict. It's one thing if I'm in a courtroom, but outside of court it's quite different."

This unusual combination of attributes—ambition, perfectionism, and extreme circumspection—helped Rosenfeldt excel as a lawyer. After Rothstein's fall and the dissolution of RRA, Rosenfeldt quickly established a new firm with the younger, former RRA lawyer Shawn Birken, where his office is adorned with plaques from thirty years as one of Florida's most honored lawyers, including a plaque that honors the "Best Lawyers in America." Rosenfeldt & Birken has its offices in the Regions Bank building on Broward Boulevard, a few blocks north of the tonier Bank of America addresses on Las Olas, where RRA was headquartered during its spectacular years. Stuart's personal workspace is also filled with dozens of citations and recognitions from charitable groups for his public service and volunteer work. This is a man still working to prove his love to an invalid mother and his goodness to a demanding father.

Many people in South Florida are skeptical of Stuart's claim that he was kept in the dark about Scott's illegal and fraudulent financial deals and knew nothing about the Ponzi scheme, but after spending more than two years of investigating, I believe his assertions are accurate. I'm inclined to believe him, even though RRA paid Rosenfeldt more than some of what the most honored lawyers in Florida earn. Although Rosenfeldt received high compensation during the firm's "boom years," I believe that, given the way RRA was growing at the time, he could have justified in his own mind the kind of money he earned during the years of growth. He was a hard-working litigator with clients of his own, and he supervised the firm's other lawyers.

Rosenfeldt has not been charged in the lingering investigation into Scott's illegal activities as many observers, including at one point even his own lawyer, expected him to be. I find Rosenfeldt's protestations of innocence credible for a number of reasons. First, as we shall see over the course of this book, Scott Rothstein was, in his own words, a "Prince of F------ Darkness," perfectly capable on his own of the greed and callousness required by the Ponzi scheme and other frauds he perpetrated. Second, Rosenfeldt's account, though exculpatory, not only has the ring of truth given what we now know about Rothstein but also is congruent with what I and others in the downtown Fort Lauderdale business community observed during the heady rise of RRA. And finally, Rosenfeldt's psychology made him perfectly suited for manipulation by Scott Rothstein, who combined in one figure the traits of Rosenfeldt's father and mother: on one hand, Scott was wounded and needy, while on the other, he was dynamic and demanding. It is no wonder that Rosenfeldt fell in line again and again, blind to behavior on Scott's part that should have put him on the alert. He needed Scott's approval, just as Scott needed his. He could ill afford to upset Scott.

"The deal from the beginning was Scott managing the firm and managing the money," Rosenfeldt explained. "I was responsible for the practice of law and supervising attorneys, making sure that quality work was being done. It seemed like the best deal in the world. Scott would personally fund the growth of the firm and I would be his fifty percent partner with equity ownership of the firm."

When Rosenfeldt told me that, sitting in his new office, I straightened up. Here was one more hint that Scott's criminality actually began before he initiated the Ponzi scheme, which is believed to be 2005. But by this reckoning, in 2001 or 2002, he was telling Rosenfeldt that he had the funds to bankroll their plans for a new law firm. "He told me that he had been in the stock market since he was twelve," Rosenfeldt said after additional prodding. "That he had all the money in the world and all I had to do was invest sweat equity and we would be fifty-fifty partners forever. Those were his words: fifty-fifty forever, and he repeated this hundreds of times over the following years."

As far as I can determine, Rothstein had made no killing on Wall Street. It was just another story, smoothly rolled out, to explain why he had more money than his law practice could possibly produce. Previously, he had told Gary Phillips that he owned some apartment buildings with his first wife, another lie. The truth is, Scott was already cheating unwary clients and skimming from settlements in employment cases.

While the friendship between Scott and Stuart was genuine,

the promise of a true partnership was not. Out from under the stifling oversight of Gary Phillips, Rothstein was free to pursue his philosophy of building the firm by hiring lawyers and merging with other firms—and by 2004, he was doing that willy-nilly, without consulting his so-called partner. Not that Rosenfeldt had a problem with the mergers and hirings on principle—he had faith in Scott's vision.

"We had a merger with Steven Lippman's firm, and with Russ Adler's firm, and Les Stracher also comes on board," Rosenfeldt recalled:

> These lawyers brought clients and gave us cross-sell opportunities, commercial clients I could sell labor and employment services to. Adler brought an entire PI (personal injury) practice into our firm. And he [Adler] had been referring cases to me for a long time. Adler also had a reputation as a great trial lawyer and we considered that important as well.
>
> Scott was always the visionary. He was the one who did those mergers. I didn't even know about them. I found out about the first major mergers when I was away camping over the Martin Luther King holiday in 2004. I was in Lake Wales with my children when my cell phone rang. It was Scott, telling me we're merging with Russell Adler and his attorneys, and Steve Lippman and his lawyers. That weekend, while I played with my children, we doubled the size of the firm overnight. In that one weekend we grew to about twenty lawyers.

During the later years of RRA, when it was the fastest growing, most glamorous, and by far the richest law firm in Fort Lauderdale, other lawyers looked on in bemusement, wondering where all the money came from. As businessman and lawyer Jim Blosser said, "I've been around law firms for forty-five years, and I know you cannot spend the kind of money they were spending. To go from zero, where Scott started, and then in the period of a year or two have the

Scott Rothstein with Russell Adler, his name partner at Rothstein Rosenfeldt Adler.

kind of economic successes to sustain the lifestyle he had and sustain the salaries of attorneys who I knew, and the money he was paying them, it was just not economically realistic."

True as that may be, however, Stuart Rosenfeldt insists that real, diligent law was practiced at RRA. The firm had significant successes and, he says, if Scott's grandiosity and greed had not gotten away from him, it could have been a legitimate leader in the South Florida legal community.

"We hit on a workers retaliation case with a $6 million verdict in 2006," Rosenfeldt said. "We had dozens of cases like that one. We had one where a man died at a fitness club where there was no defibrillator. That case was won at trial in 2005 for over $800,000. And I had enough in the pipeline that I was working continuously through the years. What distinguished us from other firms was that we were not scared of going to a jury trial," Rosenfeldt said. "We would leave money on the table if we didn't think it was enough. And we definitely built a reputation."

Rosenfeldt defended Rothstein's strategy of expanding the firm from seven to seventy lawyers as productive—if only he'd gone a little slower and paid more reasonable salaries:

> In 2005 we hired Andy Peretz for entertainment law. For health care we brought in Jeff Bernstein, who was a very successful attorney in Philadelphia. Government relations were headed up by Grant Smith. Copyright and trademark was headed up by Frank Herrera. We had a patent practice with someone who had been head of the patent department at Motorola, Gregg Rasor. Steve Lippman did commercial litigation. Les Stracher did automotive. In 2007, we began bringing in real estate people. Arthur Neiwirth was responsible for real estate and bankruptcy. We were doing great. Or at least, that's what it looked like.

In those early, developmental years, Rosenfeldt recalled, it was a joy working with Scott. "He was always happy, always upbeat and fun," Rosenfeldt said. "He was always optimistic." And yet, Rothstein's obsessive management style slowly began to grate on Rosenfeldt. "He didn't give out responsibilities. He assumed it all with respect to management functions. I would ask, 'What can I do?' And he would say, 'Get more clients.' There were committees for employee compensation, for the website, for mentors, for risk management, but it was all 'window dressing,'" Rosenfeldt said. "It would always be Scott's decision in the end."

As a manager, Rothstein was what Rosenfeldt called "a benevolent dictator." Said Rosenfeldt, "He was very generous with people, very compassionate. He had the appearance of really caring about everybody. Scott and I shared one thing, and that was never tolerating any abuse towards anyone on staff. We fired [lawyers] for abusing staff." Something that later became a source of widespread derision was Scott's habit of signing his memos and e-mails "Love ya, Scott," something that he did from the beginning of his partnership with Rosenfeldt. While some find it unprofessional, a coarse affectation, Rosenfeldt claimed it was "affectionate." But there were things about Scott's emails that bothered Stuart, particularly the penchant for vulgar acronyms.

> Sometimes he would include the letters "HMFIC," which would stand for "Head Mutha F---- In Charge." He was doing that in 2004. Then the one that really bothered me was "POFD," which I later found out to stand for "Prince of F------ Darkness." He only did that one a couple of times, because when I learned what it stood for, I went to him and I said, "Scott, that offends me because of my faith." He did not keep it up any longer. But he used these letters in memos to all the lawyers. He was always devilish. That was part of his charm.

The flamboyance for which Rothstein later became famous was present from the beginning, although it grew as time went by. For a long time, Rosenfeldt said, it was an asset for the firm. "Yes, he was always flamboyant. Scott was charming. Scott was Scott. I'd say we were yin and yang. We were opposites. He was the best guy to party with, that was his image. You'd always have fun. With Scott, you'd laugh a lot. He has a way when he meets someone, to have them like him. He was always very friendly, happy, and the kind of guy everyone wants to be friends with. He also had a great laugh."

Over time, the gleam of Scott's charm and the pleasure of being in his company dulled for Rosenfeldt. Over the years, Rothstein's flamboyance became ever more pronounced until he turned into "a caricature of himself," as Rosenfeldt said. "I thought it was silly with the bodyguards and everything. I asked him, 'Do I need a bodyguard, was there something he hadn't told me?' He said, 'No,' that he lived ostentatiously, and that John McCain had advised him to have a bodyguard. That was about 2008." It was also about the time Scott turned his suite of offices within RRA into a high-security bunker. After Scott's fall, the high-powered Miami attorney Kendall Coffey, hired to salvage the reputations of the remaining lawyers at the firm, led the media on a tour through the bunker in a successful PR stunt to show how Rothstein had separated himself from the rest of the law firm. How could the other lawyers know what Scott was up to if they couldn't even get into his part of the floor? "I had card access, but sometimes it would get turned off and I'd become upset about it," Rosenfeldt said. "Scott would apologize and say, 'It wasn't aimed at you; it was because of David Boden.' Scott would always have a different excuse for it happening."

At some point in 2008, Rosenfeldt had had enough. He had no decisions to make, no say in the firm's business operations, even though Rothstein always introduced him as "co-founder" and always spoke of "Stu and I." But Rosenfeldt felt shut out from the strategies and management of the firm. "I was not happy with the way things were going and I didn't feel like I was part of the firm like I should be." Finally, he slipped Rothstein a note saying he planned to leave and open his own one-man shop. "Scott came crying in my office and said he couldn't continue without me. He begged me to say, and for a long time after that he'd come to my office every morning and tell me about the decisions he was about to make and ask me if I had any issues or concerns." Once again, Rosenfeldt allowed Scott's charm, his winning yet needy personality, to overcome his own best instincts.

Without getting access to Scott himself—he has steadfastly refused all requests for interviews since he disappeared into the federal prison system and the Witness Protection Program—it seems impossible to determine how much of what he became and how he operated was part of an overall plan. Was he a criminal mastermind, with a grand strategy to exploit Rosenfeldt's reputation? Did he know that he could parlay his larger-than-life persona into a platform upon which he built the fastest rising law firm on the Eastern Seaboard? Did he plan to use all that as cover for a get-rich-quick Ponzi operation? Did he know he would be forging judges' signatures on bogus settlements, bilking clients, and drawing investors into a Ponzi scheme? Did he know in 2002 that wooing and politicking among the rich and influential in the trendy restaurants and bars in downtown Fort Lauderdale would help him build his image and cultivate victims? A strong case can be made that he did not. Instead, while Scott was a smooth operator, full of charm and fellow feeling, fast on his feet and fun to be around, it may be that he operated mostly on hunches and instinct. Ambitious, hungry for wealth and power, he went through those doors that opened to his touch whether they were legal or not. I don't mean to downplay his intellectual gifts, legal abilities, or his capacity for evil. He was brilliant, and as far as I can see, without remorse. I don't think he had a master plan, at least not in 2002.

I base this conclusion on, among other things, the way Scott first became involved in politics. It was 2002, when a rising moderate Republican politician named Charlie Crist was running for attorney general. Three important Fort Lauderdale lawyers, Jim Blosser, William Scherer, and John Collins, were mounting a fundraiser for Crist to be held at Burt & Jack's, an upscale steakhouse partly owned by movie star Burt Reynolds. "Scottie said, 'Yeah, I'd be interested in helping you with that,'" recalled Blosser. "He said he had some clients who would support Crist. Lo and behold, Scottie came down and it was his first venture into politics. He met Charlie Crist for the first time and became enamored of the concept of being involved with politics. It got in the blood of Scott Rothstein and we worked on a few other campaigns." But soon, Rothstein began "doing his own thing," Blosser added, cutting checks, using his own name, and "moving away from those of us who had been around with an established system of raising money for various candidates."

It was almost as though you could see Rothstein's eyes widen with the realization of how much fun becoming a political kingmaker could be and how valuable it could be for his dreams and schemes. Rosenfeldt said that Scott gained more than a taste for the perception of power that comes with politics. "He developed a vision that he wanted an entire firm that was politically connected, and that had talent working in every area." That first fundraiser at Burt & Jacks was the beginning of a beautiful friendship with Crist, a man who would eventually become governor and introduce Scott to such Republican standouts as John McCain and Arnold Schwarzenegger.

Not everyone was quite as impressed with Scott's brash charms as Rosenfeldt was, however. The former executive vice president and general counsel of Huizenga Holdings, Blosser has long been an influential player in South Florida business and legal circles. He helped Wayne Huizenga bring baseball's Marlins and hockey's Panthers to Miami. He was a local leader in Republican presidential and gubernatorial campaigns going back to 1988, including George H. W. Bush's successful run for the White House. While his first impression of Scott was favorable, he soon found the cocksure younger lawyer's style too flashy for his taste. He met Scott at Jackson's, another steak house favored by the city's influential elite.

"There was a lawyer who had just moved up here from Hollywood and was anxious to get acquainted with town people in Fort Lauderdale," Blosser recalled.

He may have had an interest in politics as well as building his law firm. So we visited a time or two in a cordial way.

I found him to be a very smart, very aggressive guy. Very self-assured. As he emerged and became more and more a recognized name in town, the brasher he became. Scottie became more aggressive, and frankly, after watching him for a couple of months, I didn't want to have anything to do with this guy. I saw he was trouble, doesn't respect anybody, and he's in this for only one thing, his own self-aggrandizement. I'd occasionally see him at Jackson's, where he'd hang out with his own entourage.

In the same way that Scott instantly saw the value of politics as a platform for his ambitions, he also enjoyed becoming one of Fort Lauderdale's most prominent boulevardiers. He loved to be seen at the trendiest eateries and watering holes, and he was always the life of the party. "He was very charismatic," Blosser said. "And probably a good lawyer if he would focus." Blosser said that Scott had the ability to make someone he'd just met feel as if they were best friends. "He had that trait. You have to have that charismatic ability to develop the network as quickly as Scottie developed his network, which goes along with his confidence and personality, which makes you feel warm. 'I want to be your friend, so please be mine.'"

Rothstein had a genius for working the restaurants and bars where the rich and powerful hung out. I witnessed many times his talent for exciting and charming people with his big, good-time personality and laser-like focus. He was always the life of the party, and his energy, charisma, and humor drew people in. He had that knack for creating a scene, in the 1960s sense of the word, and it was a scene of which onlookers instantly wanted to be part. Not only did the atmosphere make you believe that he was important but also it allowed you to feel more important once you were a part of it. I was able to quietly resist, and so were some other people, such as attorneys Jim Blosser and Stephanie Toothaker, but many savvy and powerful people were drawn to Scott's flame. Perhaps his greatest conquest was Ted Morse of the Ed Morse

Scott Rothstein with his accountant, Tracy Weintraub.

automobile dealership empire, but his showmanship also won over some of the most powerful lawyers in town and some of the most influential accountants as well. He had a Midas touch about him. It was something to see. Scott gave the impression he was a deal maker, and if you wanted to be a part of his success, all you had to do was hang around and have a drink with him. Part of his glamour was derived from how he arrived out of nowhere and became a rich, powerful, important person almost overnight. Soon, he had such powerful friends that those of us who were skeptics were very careful about with whom we shared our doubts. The owner of a successful Florida public relations firm, I had to be cautious so as not to offend a powerbroker or be called out as a naysayer. I could not afford to be the first one criticized for not drinking Scott's Kool-Aid. Still, it was obvious to me and many others that something about Rothstein did not quite add up.

I must give Scott credit, however. In those early years, he did not seem to make even one misstep, at least not in the way he moved through the city's restaurants in search of power and connections. He first showed up at Jackson's, at

Scott Rothstein with Roger Stone. (Courtesy *South Florida Business Journal*)

the time the most elite downtown eatery. It was expensive, but if you were anybody, then you spent time and money there. You couldn't afford not to. Scott put in his time, almost always stopping in after work in 2003 and 2004 for drinks and dinner. Then, along with other powerful local players, he gravitated to the Capital Grille, a new, high-end restaurant at the Galleria Mall, about a mile northeast of downtown near the Intracoastal Waterway and the beach. The Capital Grille is where he introduced Roger Stone, the infamous Republican strategist who once worked for Richard Nixon, to Charlie Crist, remembered Stuart Rosenfeldt. "It became his new stomping ground," Rosenfeldt said. "He had lunch there all the time and was probably one of their best customers." For the next two years, Scott was a fixture at the Capital Grille. The location had the advantage of being closer to the Ed Morse Cadillac dealership, making it easier for Scott to cultivate his deepening friendship with Ted Morse.

It was there at Capital Grille that Scott solidified his image as a larger-than-life character. More than once, I heard with my own ears his declaration of his grandiose vision: "I'm taking over Florida," he would crow with a flourish, "then the Eastern seaboard. Then the world." He would let fly his big, booming laugh, but anyone who assumed that that meant he was kidding, that he wasn't serious in this ambition, did so at their peril. Some of them wound up victims in his Ponzi scheme. "As he emerged more and more as a recognized name in town," Jim Blosser said, "the brasher and brasher he became. Scottie became more aggressive. At places like the Capital Grille, he became very boisterous. Martinis at lunch and the full gamut of being a big shot. Scottie became very vulgar, very loud."

Once Scott started to make contacts by working the watering holes and by taking part in Republican political fundraising, he was able to rub shoulders with such important local figures as Wayne Huizenga, Justin Sayfie (Blosser's partner and a former speech writer for Jeb Bush), and many others. Not all of these powerful people were taken in, such as the unfortunate Ted Morse, but neither could they avoid him altogether, not when he was bringing in significant contributions to Republican-party coffers. These connections, in turn, allowed Scott to project an image of success and power, which later helped to recruit some of the best and brightest attorneys in South Florida to RRA, including former judges. The firm may have been a hall of mirrors— the illusion of success leads to political connections, which enhances the illusion of wealth and power, which in turn attracts top talent—but it was deftly executed. Once RRA started to make a name for itself, Scott was positioned to set up the Ponzi scheme. That's when the real money started to flow, and with it came all the advantages it could bring: real estate, luxury cars, a multi-million-dollar watch collection, and an unending bevy of strippers, escorts, and gold diggers. Said Jim Blosser, who has been involved in Florida business and politics since the 1980s, "His rise to recognition and power and influence was unmatched in anything I've seen."

Chapter 3

Scott Steps Out

Scott Rothstein began to spend big money in 2003, buying cars, clothes, and jewelry. Previously, he had managed an expensive car or two—he knew and valued the importance of image—along with some nice clothes and a flashy watch. But by early 2003, he ascended to another level, wearing expensive suits from Moda Mario, the exclusive clothing store on Las Olas Boulevard, among other high-end local establishments. The timing of this uptick in lifestyle raises an important question: if Scott Rothstein financed the bulk of his extravagant spending by means of the Ponzi scheme, which got underway in 2005, where did he get the money that he spent in 2003?

Scott Rothstein has been secreted away in a prison since the summer of 2010, his whereabouts known only to federal officials, as he serves the fifty-year sentence handed down for his crimes. The efforts to recover money for bilked investors continues, as led by Herbert Stettin, the attorney chosen by the bankruptcy court as Chapter 11 trustee for the dissolution of RRA, as well as by William Scherer and three dozen other lawyers representing individual investors and groups. In December 2011, the Justice Department allowed Scott to emerge for two weeks of depositions with investors' attorneys in a Miami courtroom, one of the most informative exercises since the Ponzi scheme had been revealed two years prior. The process of recovering investors' lost funds will continue for years. In May 2011, Scott's empty lot across the street from the Harbor Beach mansion where he lived in gimcrack luxury with his second wife, Kim, sold at auction for $1.8 million. A spiffy, two-bedroom condo in Midtown Manhattan, which the Rothsteins bought in the glory days of 2008, went on the market for $5.4 million. Scott paid $5.95 million for it. And Stuart Rosenfeldt, who may have been guilty of nothing more than poor judgment and gullibility, settled a $10 million clawback lawsuit by the bankruptcy trustee for $1.6 million.

The fallout from Scott's orgy of fraud will continue for years, doubtless growing ever more baroque as it goes. For example, Rosenfeldt, accused of receiving excessive compensation while working as a partner at RRA between 2005 and 2009, will pay the settlement out of a $3.97 million refund he's expecting to receive from the IRS. Rosenfeldt received a Maserati from Scott, which he later returned. He told me during an interview that he didn't want the sports car and never put more than five hundred miles on it, leaving it parked in the garage at the Bank of America building. "All that largesse," said the trustee, "had to have come out of Rothstein's Ponzi scheme."

Many local observers were left scratching their heads that Rosenfeldt came out of this scandal with the Internal Revenue Service owing him almost four million bucks. Other Byzantine arrangements are sure to come to light. I say that not just because the case itself is so complicated, but also because, well, that's just the way things are in South Florida—odder, weirder, crazier than even in big cities. It's no coincidence that the proto-reality show *Cops* began in 1989 by following the Broward County Sheriff's Office, while a popular current show on the cable channel TLC is entitled *Police Women of Broward County.*

In the beginning, Scott was not as extravagant and melodramatic in his dress, his spending, or in his persona as he would become later on. As Amy Howard, a manager at Capital Grille who later went to work at RRA, told

Investigative Discovery, "I guess as the business grew for him, so did his persona. It just kept getting bigger and bigger." There was a build, an evolutionary arc to this rogue's progress. According to the *Miami Herald,* Scott's net worth soared from $160,000 in 2003 to "tens of millions of dollars" six years later just before the fall. As far as I can tell from property records, Scott's first big purchase came in 2003—at least two full years before the Ponzi scheme was supposed to have been initiated—when he bought a house on Castilla Isle in the prestigious Las Olas Isles neighborhood, just west of the Intracoastal Bridge that leads to Fort Lauderdale Beach. It's an old Florida/new money neighborhood with modest homes with beautiful architecture mixed together with fantastic estates like that of Wayne Huizenga, a few isles over, which takes up an entire block. Scott bought the Castilla Isle house one day after the sale of the suburban Plantation home he had bought with first wife, Kimberly Hill, in 2001. On paper, Scott and Kim No. 1 made a profit of $200,000 on that sale to accompany the $40,000 they cleared on the sale of a Plantation condo the year before.

Nothing was ever enough for Scott as he rose in wealth and prominence. In 2005, he bought another Castilla Isle house, this one previously owned by Miami Dolphins running back Ricky Williams, for $2.73 million. After moving into Williams's prior home, Scott bought two more houses on the same street. "They call me the king of Castilla," he liked to joke.

Let me say here that in referring to Scott's first wife as "Kim No. 1," I mean no disrespect to Kim Hill, who was out of the man's life long before he became the caricature splashed across newspaper headlines and television news shows around the country. She has steadfastly refused to comment on Scott's travails with any reporter or writer, including me. While I'd love to know what she remembers of Scott's character during the ten years they were married, I can only admire the wisdom of her decision to choose the dignity and privacy that is best preserved by silence. Today, Kimberly Hill is a respected lawyer specializing in workman's comp defense for a medium-sized civil litigation law firm in Deerfield Beach, a few miles north of Fort Lauderdale. I reference her as "Kim No. 1" only because both of Scott's wives were named Kimberly, though otherwise they could not have been more different—a curious and meaningful fact. Of course, Kimberly is not an uncommon name, and it might be a matter of mere coincidence. But I can't help but wonder if this coincidence does not offer some glimpse under the lid of the Pandora's Box that is Scott's brain, personality, and character.

Kim Hill divorced Scott in 2003. As both were modestly successful workaday lawyers, I presume they split the proceeds from these two real estate transactions, which would have left Scott with $120,000 to sink into his new digs in east Fort Lauderdale. Records reveal that Scott carried an initial mortgage of $885,000 in the neighborhood of what you would have been left with after a $120,000 down payment, which suggests that at the time, he was still organizing his finances as everybody does. As the *Miami Herald* reported in 2009, at the time of the divorce, Scott and Kim No. 1 shared stocks and retirement plans valued at a mere $206,000, which they agreed to split. "Barely prosperous, let alone affluent," is the way the *Herald* described Rothstein's situation in 2003.

And yet, based on my observations of Scott, I believe he already had some kind of game plan, and that million-dollar Castilla Isle house was one of the first few steps in moving it forward. I see evidence that Scott had already started to indulge in sharp business practice and even outright fraud and criminality in order to finance his ambitions by this time. Greed may have gotten the better of Scott as time went by and, after the Ponzi scheme was up and running, more and more money was flowing in, but he was behaving like a con artist before then. Looking the part of the energetic, creative, and rich entrepreneur was key. That's why, apart from greed and pure pathological acquisitiveness, he bought cars, watches, motorcycles, yachts, and ridiculous hand-made suits and such extravagant tchotchkes as golden toilets for the Harbor Beach mansion he would share with Kim No. 2. As US Attorney Jeffrey Sloman told *Investigative Discovery,* "That was part of his plan. To look successful, to be wealthy, to be politically connected. That was all part of his scheme." And while Scott probably didn't have the scheme sketched out in detail as early as 2003—I doubt he knew yet that a Ponzi con was going to be part of it—he most certainly was already cheating clients. As we know from Mark Booth, Scott won an employment discrimination case for a pregnant woman fired from her job, then kept the news—and most of the money—to himself. The case was won in January, 2000. Scott was an equal-opportunity thief, stealing from the rich and powerful as well as the down-and-out and powerless. During his bankruptcy court testimony in December 2011, he referred to himself as Robin Hood: "I steal from the rich and give to the richer."

Consequently, Rothstein stole from those he considered friends. Consider Ed Morse, a World War II veteran who built a car dealership empire in Florida. In 2006, Morse and his wife, Carol, hired Rothstein to sue an interior designer in a $2 million dispute over work done at a condo in Boca Raton. Three years later, in 2009, as the Ponzi scheme began to fly out of control and Scott became desperate for money to keep it spinning, he told Morse that he had won the case plus $21 million in punitive damages. Unfortunately, the defendant had, according to Scott, moved the money offshore, and Morse had to post a bond for two and a half times the judgment—$57 million—before the money could be returned to the United States. In fact, Rothstein had lost the case and accepted a settlement that obliged Morse to pay $500,000 to the interior designer. To fool his client into wiring him the $57 million, Scott fabricated court orders and forged the signatures of two federal judges. One of the orders imposed a "strict confidentiality" agreement, threatening severe penalties that kept the Morses silent even after they started to develop suspicions. This swindle was not part of the Ponzi scheme— but its purpose was to support it. As Scott testified in 2012,

> I'm confident as I sit here today that every one of the tentacles of the criminal enterprise that I was running, all flowed back in some way to benefit the Ponzi. Whether it was power in any phase, judiciary, law enforcement, banking. Whether it was laundering money for organized crime and all the myriad of things that occurred in between. They were all involved, at some way ultimately funding or assisting the Ponzi scheme.

Morse considered Rothstein a friend as well as an attorney, and as everyone in town knew, his son, Ted, was Scott's best friend. Yet none of that mattered. Nothing stopped Rothstein from stealing.

I think it's very likely that Scott engaged in this kind of chicanery, probably on a smaller scale, for a good decade before the Ponzi scheme went bad on him. Remember, he told Stuart Rosenfeldt he could finance the new law firm, claiming he'd done well with investments. Instead, I think he was cheating small clients, like the drug-addicted waitress, out of their judgments and settlements. It seems as if Scott was willing to cross ethical and moral lines to get what he wanted well before he cooked up his grandiose Ponzi fraud. It may be that it was only a matter of scale, that as time went by without his getting caught, Scott grew bolder. Or it may be that his ethics degraded incrementally with each con that succeeded, making him willing to run bigger risks the next time. Or it may be that by the time he pilfered the $57 million from Morse, he had grown desperate to keep the Ponzi pyramid standing. Scott knew that once he ran out of money and could no longer pay the oldest investors, the whole, shaky edifice would come crashing down on him—which is exactly what happened in November 2009.

But while I'm convinced that Scott was engaged in illegal and unethical activity prior to 2005, I think it's important to not let our imaginations run away with us. Fortunately, we don't have to. Examples of Scott's misdeeds abound. For example, consider his representation of Whitney Information Services Network, a collection of companies founded by get-rich-quick guru Russ Whitney. Not exactly a paragon of business honor himself, Whitney was variously termed "a real estate infomercial guru" and a "suspected swindler" by reporters covering the aftermath of Rothstein's fall from grace. Whitney claims to be a self-made millionaire who parlayed a thousand-dollar investment into a $4 million real estate empire in only eighteen months, beginning when he was twenty-five. Through his various related educational companies, he offers to train others in his investment strategies. According to the *New York Times,* which profiled Information Services Network and its related companies in a March 18, 2007, story, Whitney entices clients with a free training workshop that is in fact a sales pitch for the so-called "Millionaire University" or some similar training program costing thousands of dollars. One woman mentioned in the *Times* story was moved to buy four training courses at Millionaire, adding $18,000 to her existing $130,000 credit card debt. Needless to say, when Whitney graduates fail to emulate the founder's success in turning real estate into a source of fabulous wealth, they turn peevish, sometimes complaining to authorities. Whitney businesses have been the subject of investigations by attorney generals' offices in Virginia, Tennessee, Florida, Pennsylvania, and Kansas.

By 2005, the Florida attorney general's office was "flooded

with complaints by suspected Whitney victims," according
to Bob Norman in the *Broward-Palm Beach New Times*.
Whitney's attorney since 2003: Scott Rothstein. A former RRA
associate told Norman that Scott personally took all calls from
the attorney general's office regarding Whitney. At that time,
Scott's new friend Charlie Crist had been elected the Florida
Attorney General. Rothstein poured money into Crist's political
career, first in the run for the AG's office, and then in the successful gubernatorial campaign. Whitney also contributed a lesser
amount to Crist's campaign in 2006. Norman's source believed
but could not prove that Rothstein used his influence with
Crist to get breaks for Whitney in the investigation. Ultimately,
however, Scott was frustrated that he could not use his friendship
with Crist to get the Whitney investigation dropped altogether,
according to Republican political consultant Roger Stone,
who had an office at RRA at one point.

Scott Rothstein with Governor Charlie Crist.

"Rothstein doesn't have any [politicians] to roll on," Stone told Norman in November 2009. "Scott was all about the appearance of influence, not influence itself. There was somebody in the AG's office that Rothstein was working with, and Rothstein got an enormous amount of documentation [regarding Whitney] to this person. But he was extremely disappointed that this attorney general's investigation kept on going despite his efforts."

Apparently, Whitney didn't appreciate criticism, resorting to litigation to make it disappear. In 2002, he sued rival real estate expert/consumer watchdog John T. Reed for trademark infringement and libel over some mild criticisms in a Reed newsletter. The main result of this action was to annoy Reed into launching a personal investigation that uncovered numerous lies and inaccuracies in Whitney's personal story. Acting as Whitney's attorney, Rothstein launched a series of nuisance or SLAPP (strategic lawsuit against public participation) suits aimed at silencing Reed by means of the burdensome cost of defending himself in court. Reed was not so easily cowed, however, and over the next few years, until the suit concluded with a confidential settlement in 2005, Rothstein and Whitney resorted to sometimes silly delaying tactics. The most outrageous may have been in June 2005, when Rothstein filed an emergency motion to postpone depositions because he had to go on a long-planned European cruise. This followed an earlier occasion when Rothstein sought a delay because he was sick. Scott's motion in connection with the cruise read, in part: "If the brief continuance is not granted, Mr. Rothstein will either appear at the depositions or lose an important client damaging his law firm. If he appears, he will lose all of the money for the trip, flights and hotels." It is amusing to consider that Scott actually thought this argument would have any weight with a judge. As the South Florida Lawyers blog remarked, "Can you believe this was actually submitted to a federal judge? On an emergency basis?" The judge denied the motion and ordered the depositions to proceed as scheduled. A short time later, Whitney and Reed reached a confidential settlement. "Maybe the best part of this story is that Rothstein was apparently counsel for the cruise line and presumably could have changed the date if he really needed to," observed the lawyers blog.

It was probably inevitable that Whitney and Rothstein would find themselves, sooner or later, suing one another. In 2002, Whitney partnered with a Panamanian corporation to develop 830 acres on the Pacific coast of Costa Rica. I don't know how much development actually took place—not much, according to some sources—but Whitney ran afoul of his partners. He hired Rothstein to sue shareholders, lawyers, and contractors who were trying to "wrest away" his stake in the development company. Among those Rothstein sued were Susan Weiss, a former Whitney student, and a Maryland businessman named Barry Strudwick. Before filing suit, however, Rothstein set up a website accusing Strudwick of "being busted for conspiracy, fraud, civil RICO, racketeering, and mail fraud," according to a *Daily Business Review* story that ran December 17, 2009. Rothstein also allegedly distributed brochures making similar charges at hotels in Costa Rica where Strudwick's clients were likely to see them.

The result of all this unorthodox legal activity: Strudwick sued Whitney and Rothstein for defamation. After settling for $3.8 million, Whitney was reluctant to pay for RRA's services. In the summer of 2009 Scott sued Whitney's companies to recover $400,000 in legal bills. Whitney, in turn, sued RRA for legal malpractice, but, alas, waited until after Rothstein had been disbarred and jailed, his assets turned over to the government, and RRA had been closed down and turned over to the bankruptcy trustee.

The Whitney suit, seeking to recover the $3.8 million

settlement paid to Strudwick, is only one of "at least three legal malpractice cases pending against the firm or its attorneys," according to the *Daily Business Review*. One of the others is from Ed Morse, suing Rothstein, Rosenfeldt, and four other RRA attorneys for malpractice in the cases surrounding the interior decorating dispute, in which Scott stole $57 million. Another is by Prince International Ventures, alleging conflict of interest "among parties the firm was representing."

These cases illustrate the fast and loose ways in which Scott conducted his business even apart from the Ponzi scheme. We may look at the Ponzi fraud now and wonder how he could have ever thought it would last more than a few years, but Scott suffered from a delusion (a flimsy, ill-supported one) that he was infallible. His sense of entitlement, exacerbated by the sense of importance he got from friendships with powerful figures such as Charlie Crist and John McCain, gave Scott the illusion he was a highflier, a rock star, who did not have to bother with the tedium of filing papers and staying on top of the details. Why should you have to bother with that when you can get the attorney general on the phone anytime you want? Why file suit when you can outsmart your opponent by spreading falsehood on the Internet? Scott operated in an atmosphere poisoned by his expanding ego and the accompanying conviction that he was above the rules that governed ordinary lawyers—that he was above the law itself.

A final example: a former Plantation neighbor, David Welch, trusted RRA with a major litigation that Rothstein promised would bring "at least a million dollars" to his client. Welch, who owned a thriving legal-staffing business, turned to Rothstein after falling victim to identity theft. In 2008, a NASA software engineer, using a computer at Kennedy Space Center on the second floor of the Joint Operations Building, used Welch's personal information to apply for loans and credit card applications. These acts constitute a third degree felony, but the engineer, Kevin Landivar, was apparently motivated not by greed, but by a desire for revenge. Welch's former landlord, he thought Welch should pay $200 to list a house he was renting with a real estate agent, who happened to be Landivar's brother-in-law. Welch disagreed and ended his lease without paying.

After Landivar stole his identity, Welch saw his credit score drop almost two hundred points overnight. Suddenly he couldn't make payroll or pay taxes or utility bills. His plans for opening a court reporting business were derailed. "I live and die by credit lines," Welch told me. "This is the worst thing that I've ever gone through. It's devastated me. When I tell you almost lost my business, I'm not exaggerating. I was literally days away from saying I've got to close the business down."

Rothstein rode to the rescue of his friend and former neighbor, repeatedly promising a million-dollar settlement from Landivar's employer, Space Gateway Support, and its parent companies, Northrup Grumman and Wackenhut Services. As usual for Scott, he was slow to resolve the litigation. Welch eventually hired an information technology expert, who traced the source of the identify theft to the NASA computer. NASA officials passed the buck to the Office of Inspector General, which directed Space Gateway Support to investigate at the Kennedy Space Center. A forensics technician found evidence on Landivar's NASA hard drive. "When they found out he was taking my personal information and transferring to his home account, their firewall wasn't up and they didn't catch it," said Welch, marveling at the breach of NASA security. "What else has he sent to his home account?"

Landivar was arrested and charged with a third-degree felony. Eventually, he was fired by Space Gateway Support, losing his job as a software engineer and the high-level clearance that went with it. He also faced a five-year prison sentence and a $5,000 fine.

With Rothstein as his lawyer, Welch sued SGS, Northrup and Wackenhut looking to achieve $1 million in damages, but when the big companies outmaneuvered RRA, using stalling tactics that earned a scolding from US District Judge William Zloch, Rothstein decided the case might not have such great potential after all. The billion-dollar companies on the other side of the dispute began to hint that Welch should settle quickly and for a pittance unless he wanted to be countersued. Spooked, Welch lost all confidence in Rothstein's ability to match up against Northrup and Grumman. He settled on terms far less than the million dollars that Scott had promised before realizing how much real legal work was going to be involved.

Landivar, in the end, got off lightly with a probation sentence. But there is no doubt Welch had a strong civil case—the Brevard County Sheriff's Department and NASA's own investigators confirmed Landivar's cubicle at NASA was the scene of the crime, according to a December 19, 2008, story by Reuters. If Scott had done his job, Welch would certainly have received proper and just compensation.

But Scott Rothstein had no interest in practicing law and winning judgments for his clients. That was for lesser lawyers.

Chapter 4

Scott and His Women

For a long time after Scott Rothstein's fall, his old friend and erstwhile partner Stuart Rosenfeldt maintained a sympathetic if stunned attitude toward him. His view was not to defend Scott or think him guiltless, but his friend's positive qualities—loyalty, smarts, creativity, charm, and, above all, a knack for getting people to do what he wanted—stayed fresh in his mind. In interviews I conducted with Rosenfeldt over the first eighteen months after Scott's exposure, he clearly retained a grudging, baffled admiration and always seemed to have something favorable to say about his former partner. Gradually, as the months and days passed and the impact of Scott's malfeasance on thousands of people in South Florida and beyond has become more evident, his feelings toward Scott have hardened. In May 2011, four people, including two IT consultants and Stephen Caputi, Scott's partner in the Bova Prime restaurant, were indicted for allegedly helping to sell the Ponzi scheme to potential investors. The last of them, Howard Kusnick, a former RRA partner, turned himself in to authorities after being charged with, as the *South Florida Sun Sentinel* put it, "helping Rothstein carry out various aspects of his complex $1.4 billion fraud." In September 2011, Kusnick was sentenced to two years for his role in defrauding auto magnate Ed Morse.

Perhaps it is the accretion of damage to people who probably otherwise would not have committed any crimes, or perhaps it has been Rosenfeldt's own suffering—the $300,000 settlement with the trustee, the hit on his reputation, the wear and tear on his family life—but for the first time, Rosenfeldt's anger and bitterness found their voice after several interviews when I asked a question about Rothstein's conscience.

"Scott doesn't have a conscience," Rosenfeldt snapped.

"I think he's a true sociopath," he said, using for the first time in my presence a word others have widely applied to Rothstein. "Any fear he may have had would've been about getting caught. I don't think he ever thought about the consequences for the people he was hurting."

We spoke, among other things, about Scott's relationships with women, which were, to say the least, not only exploitative but also extraordinarily complex. He may have been a cad and a womanizer, capitalizing on unequal relationships with graduate students when he taught at Nova or clerks and secretaries and other lawyers at work, but he also had deep and lasting connections to women he did not seduce. Chief among these was Debra Villegas, the receptionist he groomed first into a paralegal, then an office manager, and finally into a chief operational officer and his indispensible right hand. In any case, Scott could not have pulled off any of his scams, including the Ponzi scheme, without the aid and comfort of the women in his life. Everything is a piece of the puzzle for Scott, supporting his greed and his ego like one big rotting tapestry.

"He did have a personality, and whatever it was, women seemed to be attracted to him," Rosenfeldt said. "He had the most engaging, charming personality. He was always fun, always laughing."

With children at home, Rosenfeldt seldom socialized with Scott—plus, his wife did not care for Rothstein—so Rosenfeldt never knew about the seamier aspects of Scott's sex life until after the Ponzi scheme collapsed and all of his former partner's secrets began to be exposed to the light of day. But he did notice at a legal seminar before the two men became partners when one of the female lawyers went to Scott's hotel room after an evening of drinking. Scott was still married to Kim No. 1 at the time. When they were about to leave Phillips Eisinger and set up their own shop in Fort Lauderdale, Scott pulled him aside to confide that he was dating Alana Cappello, a lawyer they planned to bring with them to their new firm. "He said it was important to Alana that I should know all the facts," Rosenfeldt said. "I didn't care if they were dating, so long as she was okay with it. Other than that, I didn't really have much interaction with him over who he was dating."

The escorts, strippers, and other pay-girls, the whispers of sex parties with potential Ponzi investors—Rosenfeldt said he didn't learn about these rumors until after Scott was in jail. There was a lot that Rosenfeldt didn't know, including when Scott forged his signature on a lease to expand the RRA office to another floor of the Bank of America Building. "He forged my signature on a personal guarantee," Rosenfeldt told me.

I found out about it on November 2, 2009, when David Boden came to my assistant and asked her if that was my signature. She said, "no, it wasn't." That's the first I knew about it. The irony is, if Scott had asked me to sign the personal guarantee, I would have. I didn't find out about the expansion until about ten days before we opened the Fifteenth Floor. Plenty of people knew, a lot of the lawyers knew, because they were going to get offices there. But I didn't know about it.

In fact, there was so much that Rosenfeldt didn't know that it aroused the skepticism of the bankruptcy trustees trying to recover the investors' money lost in Scott's Ponzi scheme. Quizzed under oath about sex parties, womanizing, drug use, and gambling—not only by Rothstein, but allegedly by other RRA lawyers—Rosenfeldt pleaded the Fifth, following his attorney's instructions. I think the trustees' point was not so much to imply that Rosenfeldt was part of the Ponzi scheme—it's clear that he wasn't—but that he should have known something was amiss with all the women, all the money, and everything else associated with Scott's social, private, and professional life during the time he ran RRA.

Rosenfeldt consistently maintains that he didn't know, and I find his protestations credible, even if his lack of knowledge may have been induced, in part, by the better-than-expected money he earned as Scott's partner. "I didn't even know who he was dating," Rosenfeldt said. "I found out he was engaged to Kim when he invited me to his house for the engagement party. We didn't socialize because our circumstances were so different." After work, Rosenfeldt said, he went home to be with his family, while Scott would be at Jackson's Steakhouse, Capital Grille, or Bova to hang out with buddies such as Ted Morse or to chase women.

Among the things Rosenfeldt didn't know about until after Scott's fall was the affair with Melissa Britt Lewis—even though Rosenfeldt considered her his "protégée." Lewis was the promising young attorney who became a partner in the firm and was eventually killed in an unusually brutal murder, strangled to death in her garage. She first met Scott when she was a student at Nova law school, where he was an adjunct professor. The relationship appears typical of the affairs Scott had before he gained access to the perks that only really big money can bring—he manipulated women with less experience and power into a sexual relationship. "Scott was having affairs with any student who came into the office," Paul Lazarus, attorney for Debra Villegas, told the *Sun Sentinel*. "And she [Lewis] started out as a student."

Villegas, indicted as a co-conspirator and sentenced to ten years in prison for her part in the Ponzi scheme, was Lewis's best friend and Rothstein's most loyal and valued employee. She characterized the relationship between her friend and

Bank of America Tower on Las Olas Boulevard, which held Rothstein Rosenfeldt Adler offices. (Courtesy Daily Business Review)

her boss as "inappropriate" in statements to the Plantation police. Lewis went to work for Rothstein in 1999 and followed him from one firm to the next until they lighted in downtown Fort Lauderdale with RRA. By all accounts, Lewis was a dedicated, diligent, and talented attorney who rose to become partner on her own merits, not by Scott's patronage. Although the affair did not last long, Lewis was apparently shamed by it—Villegas said that neither Lewis's family nor her friends or co-workers knew about it—and it was the reason that the rising young attorney briefly left RRA to work at another firm, Shutts & Bowen. "There were three other people in the firm Scott had relationships with," Villegas said. "It was a joke around the office that Scott had these relationships. . . . The other attorneys were always talking about it, and she just felt uncomfortable."

During Scott Rothstein's two-week deposition before three dozen attorneys in the last two weeks of December 2011, he, under questioning by attorney Sam Rabin, acknowledged his affair with Lewis when she was in law school.

Rabin asked, "Was she married at the time you were having the relationship with her?"

Rothstein responded, "No, she was a student of mine."

Lewis told her family that she left RRA because she could no longer abide Rothstein. Her aunt, Lynn Haberl, told Bob Norman at *New Times* that "she said she wouldn't work for the S-- anymore." But for a variety of reasons, she returned after only a short time. Supposedly, she came back in part to support best friend Villegas, who had been diagnosed with ovarian cancer; because she "got over" the shame of the Rothstein affair, now long in the past; and because she "didn't fit" well at Shutts & Bowen, where she found the close supervision she received as a new employee uncomfortable. Finally, she returned to RRA because her supervisor would now be Stuart Rosenfeldt, not Scott Rothstein.

It's interesting to contrast the affair Scott had with Lewis, which was typical of his philandering and readiness to abuse unequal power relationships for easy sex, and his long, complex relationship with Debra Villegas, by far the most important woman in his life and with whom he never had intimate contact. In fact, the three are a kind of ménage-à-trois—not in the sense of a sexual threesome, but more of a complex weave of friendship, loyalty, and lust. Scott seduced Lewis sexually, to her later regret, when she was a young law student, while he seduced Villegas, a working woman with a rough childhood, with mentorship, devotion, and trust, giving her increasing responsibility over the years. Meanwhile, Villegas and Lewis became best friends, as close as sisters, supportive through illness, divorce, and other ups and downs over many years as they lived and worked in Scott's orbit. They called each other "Ethel" and "Lucy." The final connection: Lewis's body, strangled in her garage in 2008, was dumped in a canal, allegedly by Debra's estranged (and possibly deranged) husband, Tony Villegas. Following the blowup of RRA and the revelations of Scott's Ponzi scheme, there was much speculation that he had something to do with Melissa's murder, either framing Tony Villegas or manipulating a psychologically unstable man into committing the act. We'll consider those theories, possibilities, and evidence further in a future chapter.

Melissa Britt Lewis is not the only young woman in Scott's orbit to meet a bad end. Julie Timmerman, a beautiful twenty-six-year-old law student who worked summers at RRA, killed herself by taking an overdose of pills on January 17, 2010, two months after Rothstein's disgrace came to light. Police insist Timmerman's death had nothing to do with the Ponzi scheme—she left a note, they said, pointing to family issues—but her life and death further illuminate what columnist Bob Norman has called "the general air of immorality and corruption" surrounding Rothstein. Timmerman met Scott through an introduction by an RRA attorney when she was looking for a college job. Through an unusual employment arrangement offered by Rothstein, she began working as a bartender at Riley McDermott in addition to a part-time clerical position at RRA. He gave her his customary onslaught of charm and money, offering to pay her tuition for law school at Nova Southeastern University, an offer she accepted. Following her death, speculation that she was another Rothstein girlfriend ran rampant, with one source "close to the firm" even telling Norman that Scott put her up in a posh downtown apartment in exchange for the usual favors.

The truth appears more complex and more sad. Although Scott paid $60,000 toward Timmerman's education, she did not sleep with him, according to lawyer Greg Lauer, husband of Julie's best friend. "She didn't know the guy was a complete d-----, and he told her, 'You go to Nova and I'll pay your tuition, and when you're done, you can come work for [RRA] as an employee,'" Lauer told Norman. "Within six months, she knew it was the worst mistake she ever made." Lauer is the person who found Julie's body, sent to her apartment by his wife after she received a series of worrisome text messages from the troubled young woman. Timmerman did work at RRA as a summer clerk for two years, but, Lauer said, she refused Scott's advances. Lauer says Rothstein took the attractive young woman out on the town as "eye candy," calling her his "little mishka" and "Jewish princess."

"She was smart enough to get a scholarship out of this guy," Lauer said. "Rothstein is such a loser that if you hang out with him, he'll give you money. He's a pig. It's disgusting, and Scott is so pathetic, you don't have to sleep with him for him to give you money." On one occasion, returning from the W Hotel on Fort Lauderdale Beach, Scott "put the moves on" Timmerman in the back of a limousine, but she rebuffed him. Lauer said that he urged her to sue Rothstein for sexual harassment, ironically putting her in touch with an employment lawyer, but she refused, saying, "He's from Brooklyn. He'll take it personally, and he'll destroy me." (Rothstein actually hails from the Bronx.) Rothstein flooded her phone with text messages apologizing for his behavior, Lauer said. Timmerman was unable to extricate herself from RRA and Scott's sphere of influence, which made it a "relief" for her when his empire crashed in November 2009.

"You don't understand. People thought it was great to work at RRA, but it was a horrible, horrible existence," Lauer told Norman. "It was a huge relief because she knew she wouldn't have to work for those dirt bags. Her suicide had nothing to do with him and the collapse of his firm." Instead, Lauer attributed Julie's death to abuse she suffered as a child, combined with "psychological issues" and "academic problems." He notes that her hand-written suicide note apologizes to her mother: "I can't live this misery anymore. I don't want to be a lawyer or anything else . . . I'm damaged. I always was and always will be and I can't live like this anymore." She closes with the hope that her father "burns in hell." Said Lauer, "She had a very hard life, but her death didn't have anything to do with Scott Rothstein." Unless, of course, she had first seen him as a surrogate father and then later as just another abuser, but that may be speculating too far.

During his December 2011 bankruptcy court deposition, Scott testified that he did in fact have a sexual relationship with Julie Timmerman. But this does not amount to conclusive evidence on the matter. Rothstein insisted to the assembled lawyers (reporters and the public were barred) that he had no reason to lie, as he had already been sentenced to fifty years in prison and his only hope in earning a sentencing reduction lay in telling the truth and helping investors regain some of their losses. Yet it is evident in the give-and-take between Scott and his questioners that he was fully in control of himself and his ego was undimmed. He bantered with lawyers, accused them of asking obscene questions (when it was suggested he had a part in the murder of Melissa Britt Lewis), and boasted about such things as his "rock-star lifestyle" and the millions of dollars he spent to supply prostitutes for himself, other RRA lawyers, and investors. While he is right that he would be a fool to lie at this point, I think Scott Rothstein cannot help himself to embellishments, and his testimony must be sifted carefully for veracity, especially when not directly related to financial crimes and the recovery of investors' money. In the case of Julie Timmerman, he has every reason to lie and very little incentive to tell the truth, if in fact the truth is that she spurned his advances. Bragging that he slept with the beautiful, delicate young woman puffs up his ego and his self-image as a ladies' man. Because his interaction with Julie has nothing to do with the Ponzi scheme or Scott's other frauds, lawyers for the bankruptcy estate and the investors were unlikely to look at it closely.

As a result, I think the version of events related by Lauer remains credible, if not certain. His portrait of Scott as a man who threw money around to buy not only sex but also the most basic human relationships does have the ring of truth. Surely not every woman Scott encountered was vulnerable to his charm. Surely not every woman was willing to sell her virtue for $5,000, or for a trip to China, or for her law school tuition. In describing her own relationship with Scott, Ms. North Beach, an established businesswoman who dated Scott for several years and requested to remain anonymous, described their relationship as "a strong friendship, and I believe he cared for me dearly." Even after they stopped having sex—she declined to continue after he married Kim—Scott remained close to Ms. North Beach. "I was a victim [of domestic violence] and he wanted to help a victim. He wanted to be the man riding on a white horse. His little chubby face wanted to help. And he did help me, immensely."

It is reasonable to suppose that that is the way Scott saw his relationship with Julie Timmerman, whether it was ever sexual or not. Julie, too, was a victim of abuse, perhaps, as he believed, at the hands of her father. Scott seems to have presented himself as some sort of surrogate father figure—but one who desired benefits. Consider this: if Scott did sleep with Julie Timmerman, a much-younger, emotionally unstable woman with known "daddy issues," then this is perhaps the most evil deed in his entire sad, sordid life. In this scenario—which is now the one Scott claims—he manipulated a fragile young woman purely for sex and thereby is directly responsible for pushing her over the edge and into suicide. While we may never know the truth of the matter, the two choices are that either Scott was a pathetic loser who had to pay to get a decent, pretty, young Jewish woman to pretend to care about him, or he was a heartless cad with blood on his hands.

Perhaps no one would be hurt more or more directly by Scott's crimes and lies, however, than Debra Villegas, forty-three at the time of his downfall. She certainly knew Rothstein better than anyone associated with the Ponzi scheme, and possibly better than anyone, period. One question that comes to my mind is why Scott never attempted to sleep with Debra. It would be easy to assume that she wasn't pretty enough to arouse Scott's lust, but that's not true. She may not have been a gym-toned woman such as Scott's second wife, Kim, but she was attractive in her own right. I think that most people would agree that she was as good-looking as Melissa Britt Lewis. Instead, a more complex dynamic played out between Scott and Debra.

Debra Villegas fled to Florida from Texas following the failure of her first marriage with two small kids in tow. "I grew up very hard in rural Texas, and my parents were not very good parents," Debra later told Plantation detectives

Debra Villegas outside of Rothstein Rosenfeldt Adler offices. (Courtesy Daily Business Review)

investigating Melissa's murder. By the time Villegas went to work for Scott Rothstein in the early 1990s, shortly after he opened his first law office in Plantation, she was a struggling young wife and mother of four kids with an abusive second husband and no college degree. She followed Scott to Phillips Eisinger and then to RRA, by which time she had risen to the level of office manager. By 2005, Scott had named her the firm's chief operating officer with a six-figure salary to match. I can't quite pin down the nexus of their relationship, but I do accept the proposition that Scott and Debra had at least the illusion of a loving, sibling-like relationship. Scott protected and groomed Debra at every stage of his progress, eventually giving her a $120,000 Maserati and a half-million-dollar house in Weston—the same West Broward development where Dan Marino lived. Scott steadily promoted Debra, bumping her salary to match: $80,000, $120,000, and near the end, $250,000 per year.

Debra depended on Scott not only financially but also emotionally. I think it probable that she grew up without a strong male figure. By supplying himself as one, Scott was able to manipulate her into doing anything he wanted. He needed someone on whom he could trust and rely, and he used Debra for that role. Being her friend and mentor was part of his game, showing that he was a good guy and a good businessman because he had someone competent and loyal with him from the beginning. When she went to the Plantation police after Melissa's murder, she spoke with Scott on her cell phone as she sat down to be interviewed by detectives. The interview room recorder taped part of her conversation: "I'm in a little bitty room with two detectives who look very scary," Debra said. "It's, ah, [Detectives] Camp and Murray . . . Yeah, very frightening. I'm gonna get shook down. I'll call you when it's over." She told police that her estranged husband, Tony, might have been jealous of the close friendship she had with Melissa Britt Lewis; he hated Scott Rothstein: "I couldn't even say Scott's name at home," she told investigators. "'Cause me and Scott are very, very close. I'm sure he hates Scott. Scott found the [divorce] attorney. Scott helped us, you know, get situated. You know, Scott pays me very well. Scott's very good to me."

What did Scott get in return? A devoted employee whose loyalty was rock solid. In the later stages of the Ponzi scheme, when Rothstein was creating documents and forging signatures, he could not have operated without her assistance. But there may have been some additional emotional connection, some deeper psychological motive for Scott. At her sentencing hearing, when she was given ten years as Scott's first co-conspirator, Debra said that she thought Rothstein was trying to "engender loyalty from me." In retrospect, she said, "I'd like to believe he loved and cared for me and was doing these things for me and the children to help us because we had nobody else to depend on." Long before the Ponzi scheme, she said, Scott "did very generous things" for her. "Even in the beginning of his practice when he made very little money, he did extremely generous things for me that I never really understood. And he always told me he believed me to be the hardest working, most loyal person he knew."

Stuart Rosenfeldt believed that Scott favored Debra Villegas because of her loyalty, a quality he greatly valued. "Debra was loyal to him," Rosenfeldt told me. "She always seemed to be the most loyal employee. They had been together for nineteen years. She started as a receptionist for Scott, same as Irene Stay [RRA chief financial officer], who was a receptionist at Phillips Eisinger. Debra was a receptionist before she became a paralegal. If Debra was unhappy, Scott was unhappy." But if some of the lawyers at RRA resented being bossed by a woman with no college degree, Stuart remembers her as highly effective in all aspects of her work. "I thought Debra was a very competent person," he said. "She was a very good paralegal; she did great work on the files she worked with me on. And she had good people skills, which Irene, our first office manager, did not have. When Irene got testy with people, Debra would work with people very well.

"Debra was a very principled person, who would always do the right thing," Rosenfeldt said, adding, "Until later, when it became known she was a willing participant with Scott's stuff."

One more woman, for yet another role, was needed to complete the image required for Scott's ambitions—a beautiful trophy wife. After dating several good-looking women around town, including Ms. North Beach and another, even closer long-term girlfriend to whom I will refer as Ms. Lauderdale (both of whom requested anonymity before they spoke with me), he settled on a tiny blonde bartender of thirty-five named

Kim Rothstein.

Kimberly Wendell. She was to prove imminently qualified for what was essentially, at least seen in retrospect, more of a job than a romantic attachment. After Scott's fall, Kim Rothstein was the target of ferocious attacks in the press, especially on Internet chat rooms and in the comments sections of stories posted online by the *Sun Sentinel* and *New Times*. Many people simply could not believe that she was in the dark, and therefore not complicit, in Scott's crimes. Others despised her for living high on what turned out to be millions stolen from other people. She was assumed to be a dumb blonde with no character, nothing but a gold-digger. While I hold little sympathy for Kim No. 2, I do have to acknowledge that in some important ways she was overqualified for the job of trophy wife, and she was immensely more complex and interesting as a personality than her detractors are willing to allow.

The circumstances surrounding the first time I met Kim No. 2 could not have been less calculated to make a favorable impression, at least on me. She showed up on Scott's arm at Bova Prime Restaurant early one evening, shortly after their

Kim and Scott Rothstein at Bova Prime.

extravagant wedding. The pair paraded around the room like peacocks, he the powerful man, she the shiny, blonde wife. She was certainly dressed for the part in an outrageously expensive outfit. I immediately pegged her as being along for the wealth, to line her pocket with as many dollars as possible while it lasted. Part of her "job description" included serving on charitable committees, and reports soon came back to me that she displayed a brittle high-handed attitude toward the other volunteers, the ones actually doing the work. Her attitude seemed to be that she was present only for show. I soon developed the same low opinion of Kim No. 2 as I'd already formed of Scott himself.

Only much later did I come to appreciate Kim's unusual qualities, and in a venue that most people found repugnant. I did, too, for that matter, but I also saw things that I had not previously noticed. It was outside the federal courthouse on January 27, 2010, the day that Scott Rothstein pleaded guilty and the day that Kim made her first public statements since the exposure of Scott's crimes two months earlier. As columnist Michael Mayo observed in the *Sun Sentinel,* everything about

Kim Rothstein reading her public statement at the Federal Court-house in Fort Lauderdale. (Courtesy *Daily Business Review*)

Kim's performance was miscalculated and off-key. Instead of lying low and distancing herself from her husband, the now-admitted despoiler of other people's fortunes and life savings, she showed up dressed to the nines, her make-up scalpel-perfect as always, in a "cream-colored Cadillac Escalade." She had in tow two lawyers, a publicist, and a bodyguard. She made an ill-considered statement in which she claimed she had not been "enriched by Scott's activities," even though she had dated him since 2005, the year the Ponzi scheme began. She said, "I have committed no crime, though the court of public opinion has decided otherwise," and decried the "unjustified slurs and accusations" raining down on her from all directions. In a particularly misguided remark, she said she was there not as "the beleaguered wife," but "to show support for Scott's parents, his victims, and his decision to return to South Florida to accept full responsibility for his actions."

I can only imagine the skepticism and outrage such words must have inspired in the minds and hearts of those robbed of thousands, hundreds of thousands, and millions of dollars by the schemes of her husband. And yet I could not help but notice the poise and steel Kim displayed in making this, her first public statement, at a time in which she was widely reviled in her hometown. Clearly, she is not without intelligence—she read her statement without a single stutter or stumble, without one pause or "uh." However ill-advised, this was the performance of a woman, gold-digger or not, making a concentrated effort to assert her dignity and reclaim her reputation.

Kim's effort, however, was the result of very poor public relations counsel. Her event ended with a physical brawl between bodyguard Joe Alu and TV reporter Rob Hambrick. Her public statement turned into another Rothstein sideshow, involving Kim live and in person. It was the worst public relations event I've witnessed in my twenty-five years of South Florida journalism and public relations. It was another case of bad judgment by Kim, or perhaps she just followed bad advice. "Kim is a very smart girl," said Ms. North Beach, one of Scott's longtime girlfriends. "I think Kim plays dumb. She has major street smarts."

At one time, the girl known as Kimberly Wendell was a local hero and role model to others. A child growing up in Plantation, the daughter of parents she later described as "very Bohemian, hippie, earthy, crunchy," she was a champion of competitive karate and a 4.0 student. That is, until she was stricken with a congenital medical condition called "arterial-venous malformation," which meant she had a tangle of oversized blood vessels in her brain. At first, the affliction was deemed inoperable and she had to give up karate while she went on medication. The side effects were so crippling, sapping her of strength and energy, that at age twenty, she elected to undergo risky surgery that could have left her paralyzed, speechless, or worse. She told Bob Norman she had had only a ten percent chance of surviving the operation intact. She came through, however, and made a complete recovery.

By that time, Kim had been on her own since age sixteen, when her parents went their separate ways. "My dad found someone, my mom found someone, and I was stuck out there," she told Norman in a *New Times* interview in early 2010. With no family support, she was left with crushing medical debt after the operation, forcing her to abandon Broward Community College, where she studied sports medicine, and work as a bartender. It was a difficult existence throughout her twenties, plagued by debt, creditors, and repo men. One roommate, paying her way through Florida Atlantic University by going on "stripping trips" to clubs in New York and Las Vegas, urged Kim to give dancing a try. "She had an amazing body," the woman told Bob Norman. "She was very tiny, about five feet tall, and weighed about ninety pounds, with these double-D boobs. She was tits on a stick. That's what we called girls like that—no hips."

Having the look is not all it takes to be an exotic dancer, however. Kim gave it a try over three nights at Diamond Dolls, a strip club in Pompano Beach. It quickly became obvious that she could not get over her self-consciousness at taking off her clothes and dancing naked for strangers. "Kim was just too sweet to be a stripper," the friend said. "Kim used to be fat, but she lost weight, and she had the mentality of a fat girl even though she was beautiful. You have to be very confident in the way you look naked on stage. She was timid like a little bunny rabbit. She was a little girl from the swamp who was sweet as a honeybee." With the easy money of stripping no longer an option, Kim drifted along in her career as a bartender, dodging creditors, dating a succession of wealthy white knights who soon revealed themselves as scoundrels of one stripe or another: one was a dope fiend, another an alcoholic, a third a conman she briefly followed to

New York. For a while in 2004, she lived and worked in Las Vegas, where her friend says she reverted to her natural look of brunette hair, brown eyes, smaller breasts, and a healthier weight. Kim worked at Light Las Vegas, a nightclub for "high rollers" that featured booze and broads, or in local parlance, "models and bottles." Kim, says her former roommate, "was still an attractive girl."

Accounts vary as to when Kim and Scott met. Some stories quote Scott, who said it was at a charity event in Fort Lauderdale in early 2005. By then Kim was thin and blonde again. But Kim told Bob Norman, in a series of *New Times* interviews at the end of January 2010, that she originally met her future husband in 2002 at the house of a mutual friend during a barbecue. Scott, she recalls, began asking her out right away, but she saw him then not as a romantic prospect but just as a customer. Her job at the time included not only bartending but also enticing men to ring up "big tabs at the drinking establishments" where she worked. Kim, who had a boyfriend at the time, said she never dated customers. She followed a boyfriend to Las Vegas, where she worked at Light, but returned to Fort Lauderdale a year or so later, after the relationship ended. Soon she had a job at Blue Martini, a trendy bar at the Galleria Mall known as a place where sharp-eyed young beauties trolled for wealthy men, and vice-versa, and she started calling old customers to invite them to come see her at the bar. Rothstein was on her list.

Rothstein immediately began asking her out again, and eventually she agreed. "He was very sweet with me," Kim said. "He was not aggressive with me. He courted me. He took things very slowly with me. He was probably the nicest person I ever dated." And he showered her with expensive gifts. Only a few weeks after that first date, Scott publically proposed during his forty-third birthday party at the Hyatt Regency Pier Sixty-Six Resort in Fort Lauderdale. She accepted. "He was the right person at the right time," she said. As her friend put it to Bob Norman, "She hit the jackpot."

But the road from engagement to wedding did not go smoothly. Kim moved in with Scott at his Castilla Isle home and he gave her a Cadillac Escalade. Scott was just then (supposedly) ginning up the Ponzi scheme. While Scott was doing well as a lawyer he was not yet rolling in other people's money. He had not started hobnobbing with political figures, and his public career as Broward County's most prominent and generous philanthropist still lay in the future. Nonetheless, he sought to control every detail of Kim's daily life. Being with Scott presented a profound challenge to the independence Kim had enjoyed since the age of sixteen, even if it had left her often insecure and in debt. "I'm used to having control over my life, over my world," she told Norman. "For someone

Kim and Scott Rothstein.

to come in and say, 'I don't want you to bartend'. . . then he would buy me clothes and he would want me to wear these things. He became like my, I don't know, my stylist? He went shopping for me. I never shopped before I met him. I hated the mall. And he would go out shopping for me. I would say, 'Does that make you happy for me to wear this? Okay, we're all happy now.'"

Given the amounts of money Kim later spent, this may be hard to credit. She certainly overcame her aversion to materialism by the time Scott's empire tilted into a flaming spiral in the fall of 2009, when Kim "shopped so much that it's now all a blur," according to a story by *Sun Sentinel* reporter Peter Franceschina. In the week before Halloween 2009, she spent nearly $5,000 in shoes from a Los Angeles boutique's website. That was the week when Scott fled to Morocco and no one knew if he would ever return. But however unseemly her taste for luxury goods, whether natural or acquired, demonizing Kim as nothing more than a gold digger or even a criminal of some kind makes it impossible to see the subtleties of her character and the complexities of her relationship with Scott. After all, she may have spent obscene amounts of money on what many of us would consider expensive junk, but other rich trophy wives spend as much if not more without being held up to public ridicule—at least not until their husbands are arrested for fraud.

"I just wanted to be loved for me, but he was in a position where he had to look a special sort of way," Kim said. "I didn't

Kim Rothstein shopping in a jewelry store.

have the clothes at the time to keep up with the Joneses, so to speak, so it wasn't necessarily out of line for him to do that. But it was mainly me not having a say in my life the way that I had. Even when I would try to sell real estate, he didn't like that."

Scott pressured Kim to get married right away, but she insisted on a longer engagement. After a time, the stress of fitting into Scott's life, just as Scott wanted, caused her to flee to North Carolina. Her mother was buying a house, and she had other relatives there, too. Kim divided her time between Scott in Fort Lauderdale, and her refuge in North Carolina, where she felt "like my old self" and take a real estate course. "I could go on a hike if I wanted to go on a hike," she said. "I could wear a pair of jeans. It could have been a way to rebel against the lifestyle he had made for me."

This arrangement displeased Scott, and he told Kim it was unacceptable. Apparently he suspected she had reconnected with a former boyfriend, though Kim said that wasn't true. Unable to get Kim to comply with his wishes, Scott turned into a bully, yelling at her and "berating" her on the phone. Kim, however, said she merely needed to assert her independence. "I'm a little hard-headed. I got my broker's license. I got a job with a developer. I got a place. I think I needed to prove to myself that I was fine, that I didn't need anyone, that I was okay. But at the end of the day, I missed this person. I was done. I came back . . . That's what happened. I came back ready to settle down. I would walk the path."

Is Kim's account credible? I think it is to some extent, though I suspect she was more calculating about Scott and obtaining access to the lifestyle his exploding wealth would afford her than she is willing to admit in this interview with Norman. "If I was a gold digger do you think I would have broken up with him?" she asks. Like everything else about Kim, this question is too complicated to yield easy answers. She fled Scott's control, true, but is that less important than the fact she returned? And when she returned she was mentally prepared to take up the job of Scott's trophy wife—to give up her independence and do things his way. "She came back a different person, say those who knew her," Norman reported. "Kim stopped drinking and became, for all outward appearances, the perfect wife."

On the other hand, while Kim was probably more of an opportunist than she wants anyone to think, I believe she was seeking more than riches and security from Scott. She wanted romance, too. I think there is ample evidence that once she gave herself to Scott, she made the compromise in her own heart to become the wife he wanted and let down her emotional defenses. The girl who was too sweet and self-conscious to become a stripper, the pretty brunette inside the hard and glittering bleached blonde façade, wanted more than the palace—she wanted the prince, too. What she got instead was essentially a symbolic post: she was to be an adornment for Scott's arm when he needed a beautiful wife for his public image. She was to represent him on charity committees and at other events he was too busy (often with another woman) to attend. She was one more valuable piece in the building up of the Scott Rothstein brand. But if Kim naively expected love, she was to be sorely disappointed. Following their lavish 2008 wedding five years after they first met at that friend's barbecue, three years after they started dating and got engaged, Scott ensconced Kim in his Harbor Beach mansion and went about his business, much of which involved chasing secretaries, waitresses, strippers and escorts.

Yet I cannot leave an impression of Kim Rothstein as little more than an innocent or neglected wife. Apparently Kim liked, or at least was willing to tolerate, fetish sexuality. After Scott's fall, virtually all of Kim's possessions along with Scott's were seized by authorities for auction, with the proceeds going to benefit the bankruptcy estate and the bilked investors. Among Kim's effects were costumes of a "country girl, nurse, cowgirl, kitty cat, wicked witch, baby doll, and angel," a Sarah Palin outfit, a Dallas Cowboys cheerleader outfit, a stripper costume, as well as the classic French maid uniform. What's more, according to Ms. North Beach, Kim liked to have threesomes with other women. "Scott said that they always used to be with other women," Ms. North Beach told me in one of three long interviews. "Those were his exact words, 'Kim likes other women.'"

Ms. North Beach told me that Scott took her to the St. Regis Resort on Fort Lauderdale beach a week before the wedding, to explain in person why he chose to marry Kim. "We had a few cocktails," she recalled, "and he said, 'I'm doing this for a reason.' I asked, 'Is this really the right thing for you?' It wasn't like he said anything like, 'I love her very much.' I got a very odd feeling, and I remember that feeling." The St. Regis was a favorite spot of Scott's, she said. "I didn't realize he brought hookers there until I read about it in the news. I was shocked."

According to a lengthy article by Bob Norman based on interviews with Bob Scandiffio, a former police officer who became Rothstein's personal bodyguard, Scott didn't usually have to chase too hard. That's because he was able to enhance his personal charm by spending thousands of dollars on any woman who would sleep with him. It always seemed to me, observing from a distance, that Scott preferred blondes, but Scandiffio said it made no difference—brunettes were fine, too, so long as they were beautiful and available. Of course, Scandiffio worked for Scott after the advent of the Ponzi scheme, when there were untold riches on tap. Norman reported that Rothstein put women up in apartments, sent them to law school, and took them on trips—he even sent one woman to China for four months.

"He gave a lot of money to a lot of girls," Scandiffio told

Norman. "And any girl he gave money to, he did. He didn't give money to anyone he wasn't having sex with . . . You take someone without money and put $5,000 in their face, they'll do what you ask them to do . . . Scott spent so much money on girls that it was ridiculous. I used to get pissed off because they were making more money than I was." And like everyone else on Scott's payroll, Scandiffio was extravagantly overpaid at $120,000 a year. At one point, he said that Scott had slept with nearly every woman working at Bova Prime, the high-end restaurant he owned with Tony Bova in downtown Fort Lauderdale.

When Scott didn't have a girlfriend or student or employee on hand, he turned to the services of professional women—strippers and escorts. Indeed, there seems to have been some overlap, with strippers and escorts sometimes resembling girlfriends, like the blond from Solid Gold, an upscale Fort Lauderdale "gentleman's club," that Scott kept at the Ritz-Carlton. "He would go into the [Champagne Room], and I would sit there and wait for him at a table outside," Scandiffio told Norman. The blonde, or let's say, the Blonde, at the Ritz-Carlton used to go drinking in the bar every evening on Scott's tab, according to taxi driver John Ciriello, who also talked with Bob Norman, spending as much as two grand a night. "At the same time, Rothstein was coming to the Ritz-Carlton with his wife and family for Sunday brunch," Ciriello said. "This guy makes me sick." Rothstein even cavorted with women on board the "Princess Kimberly," the yacht he bought and named in honor of Kim No. 2.

Scandiffio, who later committed suicide, thus becoming the third person in Scott's circle to die under mysterious circumstances, bolsters Kim's view of herself as a lonely, neglected wife who married for love. "I really felt sorry for her," said Scandiffio. "All she wanted in the world was for this man to pay attention to her, and there was nothing she

could do to get him to pay attention. It was one of the saddest
things I've ever seen. I hated it because I was paid in part
to lie to her like he was doing. It was part of the job. Kim
went [to the Ritz] one time yelling and screaming, 'Where's
my husband?' Meanwhile, he wasn't there. He thought it was
funny that she would get so freaking pissed off. She would
call his phone one hundred times, and she would call my
phone one hundred times. I had to lie to her all the time, and
I don't like to lie."

One reason Scott hired a bodyguard for Kim was to keep
track of her while he was gallivanting with other women. He
didn't want to worry about running into his wife with another
woman on his arm. Scandiffio and Kim were close friends
in the early days of her marriage to Scott, even traveling to
Disney World together with Scott's daughter—part of Kim's
job was entertaining the little girl during visitation weekends.
Scott was too busy to bother. Eventually, however, jealousy
arose between Kim and Scandiffio. As Kim told Norman,
they competed for Scott's attention. "He wanted to be the
one, the man, the person Scott went to for everything," she
said. "It became overbearing to me. I resented things, but it's
not Bob's fault. I resented that Scott wasn't there."

Said Scandiffio, "He would never say anything to her. She had
her house, she had her money, and she got her hair done every
day. He gave her a job [helping to run his properties] because
she needed something to do. She spent plenty of money, but
she wanted him to pay attention to her, and he never did. I
think she has a lot of self-esteem issues with Scott never being
home and never doing what she wanted him to do. I'm sure it
had to be embarrassing for her because everybody knew. All
his friends knew. And she loved the guy. It was horrible."

Scott's penchant for adult clubs and escorts was well
known. Or maybe I'm being influenced by hindsight. Those of
us who were paying attention in the years and months leading

An enamored Kim Rothstein with Scott Rothstein.

up to Scott's fall, who were skeptical of his overbearing style
and the source of his riches to begin with, were certainly not
surprised by the revelations that have come out about his sex
shenanigans. We did hear some rumors during his high-flying
days of a predilection for strippers and prostitutes. In addition
to what's been reported in the press, I've spoken with sources
close to Scott: business associates, personal friends, and in
one instance a former employee of an escort service who did
not want to be identified. I find it oddly touching that in our
increasingly vulgar culture, where porn stars can become
pitch models for clothing companies, celebrity sex tapes
pop up regularly on the Internet, and disgraced politicians
appear in TV commercials while awaiting trial, people are
still embarrassed to have any connection, however tenuous,
with the escort business. Some of my sources never hired pay-
for girls, never worked with or for escort services. Their only
association with prostitution is the misfortune of knowing
Scott. Yet they are too embarrassed to talk for attribution.

Be that as it may, all three sources tell a similar story,

confirming Scott's use of pay-for girls and shedding additional light into this dark and sleazy corner of his story. For starters, according to one of my sources, escorts were the chief entertainment at Scott's bachelor party just before he married Kim No. 2 on January 26, 2008, at the Versace Mansion in Miami Beach. My source, who was present at the bachelor party, says it included ten of Rothstein's closest friends and started at the Prime 112 Restaurant in South Beach, where a chopped salad is nineteen dollars, a hamburger is thirty dollars, and a New York strip steak is fifty-six dollars. The men then retired to the Versace Mansion, where they were joined by six women from Miami Companions for after-dinner festivities, the highlight of which was oral sex. Like the Cheetah Club, Miami Companions not only served Scott as a client but also hired his services as an attorney. Unfortunately, owners Gregory and Laurie Carr were unable to benefit from Scott's legal acumen, as their arrests for running what was characterized as the country's largest prostitution ring surfaced in the summer of 2010, a month or two after the disgraced lawyer was sentenced to fifty years in prison. If Scott had been free to give the Carrs better legal advice, they might have been able to sell their business before the feds came knocking.

Sources at RRA have confided to me that Scott was both an attorney and a VIP client for Miami Companions. I've also spoken with a former employee of the service, who worked both in the office and as an escort, who confirmed both points. Lurid rumors that Scott held "sex parties" in private rooms on the second floor of Bova Prime, the restaurant he briefly owned on the street level of the Bank of America building where RRA had its Las Olas offices, cannot, alas, be confirmed. These widespread (and widely believed) stories say that Scott lured investors into his Ponzi scheme by hosting orgies featuring Miami Companion girls at Bova or in the two-bedroom condo he maintained nearby at 350 Las Olas

Place. As colorful as these tales may be, and as much as it fits the old "Miami Vice" image that South Florida so likes to shun and simultaneously exploit, I find them not entirely credible. For one thing, a man with the money to invest in Scott's billion-dollar Ponzi scheme would probably be able to find female companionship on his own with little or no trouble. For another, these were sharp businessmen, such as Ted Morse and George Levin, used to paying attention to details and coming out on the winning side of business deals. It beggars belief that they could be fatally distracted from the bottom line merely by the promise of sex.

During the run-up to the disintegration of Scott's fall, when it seemed he could do no wrong and many of us around Fort Lauderdale wondered what he was really up to, I could not credit the rumors of orgies with call girls and strippers. For one thing, I did not think they were necessary. All along, in everything that he did, Scott wanted to be the big guy around town, the one with the most toys and the most beautiful women. I think Scott deceived and fooled investors by building a sexy illusion of wealth and glamour and excess. Part of it was no doubt ego compensation—a stocky fellow who once stood out only in the school choir, he did not take the Homecoming queen to the prom. But it was also classic con-artist misdirection. Scott entertained investors at Bova with plenty of beautiful women around, after which he would take them to the Cheetah or Solid Gold. The combination of alcohol and pretty women can greatly blur a smart man's judgment. That was part of his game. Just having the beautiful young women around to spice up the atmosphere and befuddle the judgment of potential investors was all he needed from them to support his con. Actual orgies were not required, or so I thought.

It turns out, as Scott testified in the December 2011 bankruptcy deposition, I was wrong. There were orgies aplenty.

Chapter 5

The Ponzi Scheme: How It Thrived

"If I wanted to screw you, I could screw you." Those are the words Scott Rothstein said at some point in every pitch to every potential investor. "If you don't trust me, you shouldn't do this deal."

No one—except, perhaps, federal investigators—knows precisely when Rothstein initiated his Ponzi scheme or whether he cooked it up alone or had backers or co-masterminds, but it was off the ground and bringing in a mounting stream of revenue by early 2005. What is known is that Scott's salesmanship was brilliant, a cocksure performance of charm, guile, misdirection, self-assurance, and the illusion of aptitude combined with expertise and insider knowledge—a confidence game in every sense of the term. His sly audacity is beautifully illustrated by that buyer-beware aside ("If you don't trust me, you shouldn't do this deal"), which must have had a profoundly disarming effect on many if not most of his potential investors. In light of all that happened after, the irony is both hilarious in a ghoulish way and almost too much to think about.

Looking back, it's stunning to think that other, very smart people were taken in by what now appears to be an astonishing array of bluff salesmanship and tissue-thin, false documentation. How savvy businessmen and investors failed to see through Scott's scheme will be repeatedly examined, but let me say here that there is more to it than the popular cliché of greed. As George C. Scott put it, "You can't cheat an honest man." While some truth may reside in that bit of Hollywood folk wisdom, a more penetrating insight can be found in a famous rule set down by the British legal historian F. W. Maitland, whose original comment is wordy and roundabout. Here is a paraphrase of its essence: always remember that events in the past once lay in the future. In other words, because hindsight is twenty-twenty, no one can claim for certain that if Scott had dangled the chance to earn, say, $75,000 on a $300,000 investment in six weeks, anyone would have had the foresight and discipline to turn him down.

That is to say, no matter how smart and successful Rothstein's victims may have been, they had never met anyone quite like Scott or seen a financial product quite like what he was selling them. Keep in mind, too, that men such as Ed Morse or George Levin or Doug Von Allmen are born risk-takers, accustomed to placing winning bets. It's in their nature to take big chances—that alpha-male drive is what has made them so successful in the first place—and it is almost beyond their imagination to conceive of the possibility they might lose, let alone be outfoxed, especially by a lawyer. Compared to the caliber of businessmen, professional investors, or venture capitalists and entrepreneurs, what does a lawyer know about business? Certainly no one expected to find a Ponzi scheme lurking in a law office. Rothstein had long told his partner Rosenfeldt that his money came from playing the stock market. Those in the community who observed Scott's extravagant wealth and knew it could not come from the practice of law (these were mostly other lawyers) suspected he was involved in some shady or sleazy side business such as Internet porn or money laundering. No one, to my knowledge, considered a Ponzi scheme or outright criminality, as in the fraud perpetrated against Ed Morse, to be part of the picture.

But Ponzi scheme it was. All it takes is for some sharp

scamster to set up an investment plan that promises returns better than what can be earned elsewhere, whether on stocks, bonds, matchbooks, stamps, collectibles, coins, gold, or just about anything that can be bought, sold or traded. In fact, often no investment or business exists at all—Ponzi schemes often work best, as in Rothstein's case, where there is only the pretence of an investment or business. Instead, early investors are repaid from the money latecomers put into the scheme. Anyone demanding his or her money is promptly paid, which, with reports of sustained high yields, creates the illusion of legitimacy, not only attracting new investors but also enticing early ones to roll their profits back into the scheme, which is what George Levin did and how he came to claim losses in the neighborhood of $700 million. (Yes, you read that right.) Although the enterprise may continue, sometimes for decades as in the case of Bernie Madoff, it is doomed, sooner or later, to inevitable failure when one of three things happens: the swindler disappears, taking a fortune of other people's money with him; the flow of new investors slows, making it impossible to sustain payments to previous investors and the operation collapses in on itself, often with panicked investors clamoring for their money; or authorities learn of the scam, arrest the principle thieves, and close the business down. As we shall see, Scott's eventual end was a combination of the latter two.

This particular kind of fraud gets its name from Charles Ponzi, an enterprising Italian immigrant who, in 1920, promised investors a fifty-percent return in forty-five days by purchasing discounted international postal coupons and re-selling them in the US at face value. Ponzi ran his scam with a brazen flair for extravagance and publicity—not unlike Scott Rothstein—and the press couldn't resist him, which is how his name came to be associated with this kind of fraudulent scheme. Investors flocked to his Boston-based Securities

Exchange Company, most of them reinvesting returns, although there was in fact no actual business taking place. Ponzi was simply paying older investors with the money coming in from new ones. One financial analyst, hired by the *Boston Post,* determined that 160 million international postal coupons would have to be in circulation to cover the Exchange's investments. In actuality, there were twenty-seven thousand. Ponzi bilked investors out of $15 million, a huge amount of money in the 1920s, before he was caught and sent to prison.

But there were Ponzi schemes before Ponzi: Charles Dickens features a Ponzi-style swindle in his novel, *Little Dorrit,* for example. In 1899, William "520 Percent" Miller took $1 million in an investment scam that promised returns of 520 percent until he was exposed by a newspaper and sentenced to ten years in prison. A woman named Sarah Howe operated a succession of Ponzi-style frauds in Boston of the 1880s, promising a high rate of return in schemes marketed exclusively to women, thereby robbing many of their life savings. She would get caught with one confidence scheme, spend two or three years at the "House of Correction," then immediately start another, similar ploy as soon as she got out, at times calling her endeavor the "Women's Ban," and others the "Ladies' Deposit."

Ponzi's spectacular fall did not deter other schemers. No, the brake on this kind of fraud did not come until the early 1930s with the collapse of an international empire developed by a Swedish industrialist and financier named Ivar Kreuger, the infamous "Match King." At one point, Kreuger controlled approximately three quarters of the world's match production. He owned legitimate businesses, too, some of which survived him, but a significant portion of his empire was based on something very like a Ponzi scheme. He amassed a huge fortune, and when it all came crashing down in 1932, his debts were greater than those of the Swedish government. He was found in his Paris apartment in 1932, the day of an important meeting with creditors, with a bullet through his heart and a pistol at his side. A note read, "I have made such a mess of things that I believe this to be the most satisfactory solution for everybody concerned." Over the decades, Kreuger's brother, Torsten, has been able to persuade some people that Ivar's death was not a suicide but a murder instead. Christopher McKenna, a business historian at Oxford University, told *Time* magazine that Kreuger's fraud was bigger than Bernie Madoff's, though he acknowledges the difficulty in comparing the two, who lived and operated in very different eras. In any event, the 1932 fall of the Match King damaged investors so badly in the United States and Sweden that it was called "The Kreuger Crash."

After Kreuger, Ponzi schemes fell out of favor with fraudsters for several decades, partly due to Congressional legislation enacted in the mid-1930s to prevent another Kreuger Crash. Late in the twentieth century, the Ponzi scheme began to make a comeback. In the mid-1980s, some sixteen hundred investors lost $50 million in the Diamond Mortgage Company/A. J. Obie scandal, termed the "biggest Ponzi scheme in the history of the state" by the Michigan Court of Appeals. Also in the 1980s, a Ponzi scheme in San Diego, operated by an investment company named J. David, stole $80 million on investments of $200 million, devastating the community and ruining political careers. Since the 1990s, when Congress rolled back legislation enacted in the 1930s, Ponzi schemes have proliferated like mushrooms. Among them is church-based scheme in Tampa that relieved eighteen thousand investors of $500 million. Pastor Gerald Payne and the elders at Greater Ministries International, citing Bible verses, promised a fifty percent return, but it was really a pretext to plunder parishioners' life savings.

The popularity of Ponzi schemes only accelerated after the turn of twenty-first century. In addition to Scott Rothstein and Bernie Madoff, one of the biggest Ponzi schemers in history, there have been a few other noteworthy men, though there are too many to list in their entirety. A part-time Scientology minister and full-time money manager named Reed Slatkin took wealthy Hollywood investors for $600 million in 2000. Nearly $1 billion was lost in 2003, when the SEC shut down Peter Lombardi's Mutual Benefits Company in (where else?) Florida, a scheme that claimed to make viatical payments to AIDS patients. Lou Pearlman, the Orlando-based boy-band impresario, responsible for the Backstreet Boys and 'N Sync, went to prison in 2006 for a $300 million Ponzi scheme that had nothing to do with the entertainment business but was based on a phony travel company. Between 2004 and 2010, grocery arbitrageur Nevin Shapiro, a Miami Beach businessman, duped investors out of $900 million in a Ponzi scheme that promised investors a ten- to twenty-six-percent return within thirty days by diverting groceries from one part of the country to another, where higher prices prevailed. And these are just the Florida-based Ponzi fraudsters, with the California exception of Slatkin, their misdeeds replicated all over the country and the world, including places such as Portugal, South Africa, Britain, Malaysia, and even Haiti, where the poorest of the poor were bilked out of $240 million in 2001—sixty percent of the island nation's gross domestic product.

After Scott's malfeasance came to light in November 2009, it was widely reported in the press that he sold investors' shares in "structured settlements." In fact, I still occasionally see references to structured settlements relating to the Rothstein case. The truth is darker and more ingenious, however, and really has nothing to do with structured settlements, which are a well-established and regulated alternative to the traditional lump-sum settlement won or negotiated by a plaintiff in a damage suit. In a structured settlement, the defendant agrees to pay a settlement in installments over a prolonged period of time, usually buying an annuity to get the obligation off of the corporate books. Structured settlements are regulated by the Internal Revenue Service because there can be distinct tax advantages for both the prevailing plaintiff and the obligated defendant. But sometimes, people who have won a structured settlement later decide they need or want more cash sooner. A lively industry exists to buy structured settlements at a discount and sell shares to investors, giving plaintiffs a lesser amount in cash up front. Investors pocket the full amount of the judgment as the payments come due, thus reaping a profit. While some unscrupulous middleman companies ply this trade, as in virtually every business, the structured settlement industry itself is completely legal and legitimate.

Scott's scheme bore some similarities to structured settlements, but only in the broadest terms. Yes, in theory people involved in damage suits were willing to sell later awards at a discount for cash now (of course, there were no such people, no such cases, no such awards, only flimflams of Scott's devising), but these products were governed neither by the courts nor by the IRS, as true structured settlements are. What's more, even if the investment opportunities touted by Scott had actually existed, they veered perilously close to extortion—gaining an odor of illegality that excited some potential investors and also provided an implicit explanation for the outlandish rates of return. After all, if something seems to be too good to be true when it comes to a rate of return, then it probably is, unless, of course, it is the fruit of sharp practice, if not an outright illegal enterprise.

Here is how Rothstein worked his scam. First, Scott was an employment lawyer, and employment law was the RRA specialty. It seemed only logical that Scott might come into possession of sex discrimination, sexual harassment, and whistleblower cases. It is also logical that big corporations or extremely wealthy individuals might, in the interests of avoiding damaging publicity, wish to settle such potentially scandalous cases not only before they could go to trial but also before they were even filed, thus keeping them out of the news. This is where the whiff of extortion comes in. Supposedly, Scott would approach a corporation or a rich individual with a potentially embarrassing allegation of gender discrimination, sexual harassment, or worse, and negotiate a big settlement in exchange for keeping quiet. Sounds a lot like blackmail, doesn't it? More than one potential investor thought so, too, and in some cases it made them less eager to sign on. Setting aside the fact that few if any of these cases were real, it is also evident how, among its many other advantages, this scheme allowed Scott to indulge his mobster fantasy, just as his uncle used to shake down the corner store.

Of course, it was not so much the details on paper that sold the investment to scores of rich, smart people, as it was Rothstein's personal energy and charm. According to Bob Norman, writing in *New Times* and citing a confidential source who claimed to be one of the bilked investors, Scott met potential investors in his "inner sanctum," the special part of the RRA office also known as the "administrative corridor" that was reserved for Rothstein and his most trusted assistants, especially Debra Villegas, the law firm's chief operating officer, and Irene Stay, its chief financial officer. In many, if not all cases, the mark—er, investor—was ushered into Rothstein's inner sanctum by David Boden, who, despite not being in possession of a Florida law license, served as general counsel at RRA and, according to Norman, "was deeply involved in the deal and negotiated the final papers with the investors' lawyers." Boden, licensed to practice in New York but not in the Sunshine State, earned $500,000 per year at RRA. At least one potential investor, North Miami Beach attorney Alan Sakowitz, was first directed to meet with Richard L. Pearson, of R. L. Pearson & Associates, a real estate firm one floor below RRA. Pearson, the "exclusive broker" for the sale of Scott's settlements, demanded twenty percent of any profits. "He felt it was a fair amount" for an opportunity to earn one hundred percent annual interest with no risk, Sakowitz wrote in his book, *Miles Away . . . Worlds Apart*. Unlike many investors, Sakowitz found the promise of such high return and low risk to be suspiciously improbable and walked away.

Everything about the approach to Rothstein's office, an impregnable suite within the larger realm of RRA's floor in the Bank of America building, was designed to impress and flatter potential investors. First, you had to gain access through a security-coded door, which closed behind you with a sigh, signaling that you had arrived in a place of privilege and power where important and lucrative work was done. Dressed in one of his $6,000-plus suits, Rothstein stepped forward to greet the potential investor with a firm handshake. If he really wanted to impress, he might show off the private elevator at the end of the corridor, disguised behind an ordinary door, which allowed him to go in and out of his inner sanctum without going through the rest of the RRA office. The other lawyers, including Stuart Rosenfeldt, never knew if Scott was in the building until they received a call or an email.

Often, an off-duty police officer stood guard outside of Scott's inner sanctum. A painting of Al Pacino in *Godfather III* hung in the private foyer just outside. His own office, spacious and luxurious with accents in mahogany and leather, occupied a corner of the building with an impressive bank of windows and a view across the downtown Las Olas district toward Victoria Park, the Las Olas Isles, the condo towers of Fort Lauderdale Beach, and the blue glimmer of the

Scott Rothstein in front of his photo-covered wall in his office at Rothstein Rosenfeldt Adler.

Atlantic Ocean. Appointed with expensive mementoes and tchotchkes, the room signaled Scott Rothstein's importance no matter what direction you happened to turn. The walls were crowded with photos of Scott doing important things: delivering giant checks to charity and hobnobbing with luminaries such as John McCain, Alonzo Mourning, county-elected officials, and Governor Charlie Crist, the biggest catch Scott had ever landed in the sea of Florida politics. On the wall hung a large painting that hid a giant flat-screen TV. Scott enjoyed showing off this technology as part of his overall pitch to new investors.

Scott had four computer monitors alight at all times. On his giant desk sat the Torah, representing the foundation of Hebrew law and displaying his devotion to the Jewish faith. A round sign on the desk read "A good lawyer knows the law. A great lawyer knows the judge," an apt maxim for a lawyer who hired judges at his firm, helped appoint them, bought them off, and, when all else failed, forged their signatures.

Scott Rothstein behind his tchotchke-laden desk.

Scott's spiel was an expert conman's sales pitch. Ironically, he used the term "structured settlement" even though he knew he was not selling structured settlements at all but pre-settlement funding. He must have thought his pigeons would be more familiar with the notion of a structured settlement, thus making his pitch more attractive. He often began by declaring that RRA was "the preeminent sexual harassment law firm in the country." He claimed that he was representing "numerous" underage girls who had been involved with Jeffrey Epstein, a billionaire financier in Palm Beach. Beginning in 2005, Epstein had been accused by as many as forty women of manipulating them into giving him erotic massages and having sex with him while they were minor teenagers. He was convicted of soliciting an underage woman for prostitution and, beginning in 2008, spent thirteen months in the Palm Beach County Jail. At least two of the young women have filed $50 million lawsuits against Epstein, alleging he had sex with them when they were underage. Citing a real scandal such as this one, especially one with a high a profile as the

Epstein imbroglio, bolstered Scott's sales pitch. After all, Epstein was known to be a friend of Bill Clinton, Prince Andrew, Katie Couric, Ehud Barak, Woody Allen and George Stephanopoulos, almost all of whom stood by him after he served his sentence, emerged as a registered sex offender, and paid millions of dollars in settlements to at least seven of the women who made claims against him.

Piggybacking on the success of attorney Gary Farmer, Rothstein also claimed to have a steady supply of settlements from whistleblower cases. Farmer worked as a name attorney on the team that negotiated the biggest whistleblower settlement in history, the $1.4 billion case in which drug manufacturer Eli Lilly & Co. pleaded guilty to charges of promoting its drug Zyprexa for applications not approved by the Food and Drug Administration. Zyprexa is an antipsychotic approved to treat schizophrenia and acute mania, but Lilly promoted its use for the treatment of anxiety, depression, dementia, sleep problems, irritability, and other mood disorders or related maladies, including those seen in children.

Lilly's abuses—promoting the drug directly to primary care physicians who do not ordinarily treat patients with psychiatric disorders—came to light only because four former Lilly sales reps filed separate qui tam suits against the company. A "qui tam" case is one in which whistleblowers are allowed to share in any monetary penalty assessed against a guilty defendant, which meant the four former sales reps received substantial chunks of that $1.4 billion settlement. Farmer worked on the case before he came to RRA, but the luster of this legal triumph came with him. This enabled Scott to take some of the credit for the case and to wield it as evidence of the firm's skill at extracting big money from corporations willing to pay to avoid publicizing their bad behavior.

Scott also bragged about the former customs agents and police officers whom he claimed worked as investigators for the firm. He told one investor that the firm's best information came from digging through garbage. Rothstein claimed he met potential defendants in his office, where he questioned them about, say, an inappropriate romance with an employee who was fired after the affair went sour. When the rich defendants denied the allegation, Scott lowered a large painting to reveal a flat-screen TV mounted on the wall. He played a video of the man having sex with his mistress. "We can depose your wife, your mistress, your daughter, and your son about it."

Of course, these were merely the stories Scott spun for his potential investors. He actually did none of these things. Scott even told an origins story, explaining how he had stumbled upon the investment potential of pre-trial settlements. It all began, he said, when a defendant in a big sexual harassment case, on the hook for a $3.5 million settlement, refused to pay upfront. Furious, Scott's client demanded they proceed straight to trial. The resourceful Rothstein, seeing his million-dollar fee disappearing, assigned the settlement. "I called up a good friend of mine in the car business" to fund the pre-settlement, Norman's source recalled Rothstein as saying, "I ask the client, would you take $3 million now. She said yes, and the settlement idea was born." Simple math shows that the original investor, putting up $3 million against an eventual $3.5 million settlement, stood to pocket a half-million-dollar profit.

With every potential investor, Rothstein claimed to have a huge Eli Lilly-style whistleblower case in the works. Or perhaps a sexual harassment case, in which an executive dumped his mistress and then had her fired in the bargain. Or something similar to the Epstein situation, in which a wealthy man was threatened with lawsuits involving underage sexual partners. In any event, the case was so sensitive that he could not name the company or the individual defendant. In many cases, Scott told potential investors, a company facing a whistleblower suit had to worry about the government mounting an investigation similar to the one in the Eli Lilly case. That is one reason executives were willing to confer generous pre-trial settlements on the plaintiffs: to keep government regulators or investigators in the dark. One investor even asked Scott if this all did not seem like some kind of legal extortion. "That's not what I'm doing," Rothstein said piously, "and that would be unethical."

At this point in the pitch Scott would brandish a legal document establishing the case and the investment, a brilliant piece of con artistry. Unlike most legal documents, the ones Scott prepared for his investors' perusal are written in relatively clear and direct language, with just enough legal jargon to remind the investor that he was dealing with lawyers. This could be enormously flattering, implying that by understanding the document, the investor stood on an even playing field—and no one is more susceptible to flattery than powerful men who already think excessively well of themselves.

Everything about Rothstein's sales pitch was brilliant, but the one real stroke of genius was the mandate for secrecy. Scott showed potential investors legal documents with the details of the case, but all of the relevant information—from the names of the companies to the names of the plaintiffs—were redacted. Indeed, he told potential investors that if the facts of the case became common knowledge, the defendant could go to court and block the payout of any remaining installments on the settlement. This was of particular concern to investors, who had already paid off the plaintiffs and now wanted nothing to interfere with the disbursement of the settlement funds. In Scott's benefit, it prevented investors from conducting due diligence on the case in which they were investing.

Sometimes, Scott brandished additional documents to make the deal appear more legitimate. In some cases, Scott flourished letters signed by TD Bank Regional Vice President Frank Spinosa, confirming the proceeds of the settlement had been deposited in a trust account. Potential investors found the involvement of TD Bank "reassuring," Norman reported. Investors who went to the trouble of investigating Rothstein's finances could only be impressed by his large property holdings and good credit history. RRA stood up well to scrutiny, too.

Some observers have wondered why investors would believe that a company paying out a settlement would put the entire amount into an RRA account at TD Bank, while insisting the obligation be paid out in monthly installments over a short period of time. Why not just pay the plaintiff a lump sum? Scott had an answer for this: tax considerations, for one thing, but it also gave the defendants a weapon to enforce the confidentiality of the settlement agreement. On the other hand, observers have questioned why plaintiffs would insist on reduced immediate cash payments, when they could reap the entire settlement if they just waited a few months to a year. For example, Sakowitz was offered a veritable menu of cases he might invest in, among which were three $900,000 settlements that could be bought for $660,000 each. The settlement called for three $300,000 monthly settlements. Sakowitz couldn't help but wonder why a plaintiff would "sell a stream of $300,000 per month for three months at such a steep discount," he wrote. "The actual return was 207 percent per annum."

Apparently, many investors were too blinkered by the Scott Rothstein show, not to mention the opportunity to make such stupendous profits, to think as clearly as Sakowitz did. While officials at TD Bank and Gibraltar Bank were later alleged to be complicit in Scott's schemes, at the minimum for allowing millions of dollars to be transferred in and out of accounts unchecked, without regard to banking regulations, this was not enough for Scott. He paid two RRA IT specialists, Curtis Rene and William J. Corte, $5,000 each to build counterfeit bank websites. Rothstein used these to prove to investors, many of whom kept rolling their money over in Scott's scheme, never taking profits, that the TD Bank and Gibraltar accounts were flush with tens of millions of dollars. As William Scherer, a lawyer representing some of the biggest bilked investors and groups, later said, "Every investor I spoke with said, 'But the money was in the bank.'" Scott also enlisted the aid of longtime friend Stephen Caputi, a partner with Rothstein in the Pembroke Pines nightclub Iguana, to sit in on some meetings with investors. Posing as a TD Bank executive, he presented bogus bank statements showing trust accounts fat with cash sufficient to cover their investments. He also, on occasion, impersonated a plaintiff.

At bottom, Rothstein's swindle had the elegance of a Nigerian Internet scam: put up some money now for the promise an amazing payout later. Some of the most intelligent and successful businessmen in the country fell for it.

Chapter 6

Building Credibility through Philanthropic Abuse

In October 2007, Scott Rothstein was the subject of a splashy profile in a society magazine called *Las Olas Lifestyle*. Like others of its kind, this publication focuses on wealthy philanthropists and socialites, in this case, the ones living and acting on the east side of Fort Lauderdale. There are lots of glossy, full-color spreads of well-dressed men and women pausing between drinks and hors d'oeuvres at fundraisers, parties, and society balls.

In this particular issue, the main story featured huge photos of a beaming Scott in various poses at his palatial Harbor Beach home. The cover showed Scott standing stiffly in the marble foyer, dressed in a ridiculous Dick Tracy pinstriped suit with the Florida sun visible through the windows at his back. He had a tentative half-smile, like a twelve-year-old boy hoping to make a good impression. A photo of Scott standing with Kim, his wife of less than a year, seemed intended solely to highlight the gigantic diamond on her left hand, draped conspicuously over Scott's shoulder. There was picture of Scott, guitar in hand, standing before portraits of Jimi Hendrix and Stevie Ray Vaughn, in addition to smaller photos of Scott sandwiched between Governor Charlie Crist and Senator Mel Martinez, Scott and Kim posing like Barbie Ken in casual affluence, and Scott grinning with a cigar. The title of the story read "A Passionate Philanthropist."

I don't mean to give the wrong impression of *Las Olas Lifestyle*. Society magazines serve a purpose in recognizing

Scott Rothstein in his Harbor Beach home.

Scott and Kim Rothstein, flaunting the diamond ring.

Scott Rothstein with his guitar, in front of portraits of Jimi Hendrix and Stevie Ray Vaughn.

the people who do genuine good by supporting various causes. Such publications have their distinct niche and readership. I've known the publisher, Jim Norton, for years, and my own photographs have appeared in this magazine from time to time from one charity event or another. Candice Russell, the writer of Rothstein's piece, has been a prominent arts writer and critic in South Florida since the 1970s, when she became the *Miami Herald*'s theater critic right out of college. This article and its photographs are important to developing a well-rounded picture of Rothstein due to the way it illustrates one of Scott Rothstein's greatest achievements: his manipulation of philanthropy and political contacts to buy social respectability and influence while burnishing his image as a wealthy and important personage—one with just enough idiosyncratic flash to feed his ego and allow him to stand out from the crowd of other rich do-gooders. One of the primary ways that Scott managed his meteoric rise in power, influence, and local celebrity, observed veteran local lawyer Jim Blosser was by "spending money and buying influence. Buying influence with charities. Buying influence in the political process. Buying influence with the appearance of a lifestyle with the big yacht and the cars and the house."

It was genius, in some ways, this three-pronged strategy, and so long as the money flowed, it worked like a dream. If Scotty could have kept the money rolling in and out of the Ponzi scheme, he could have dominated philanthropy in South Florida forever, building an ever-grander empire with more and more awards and buildings bearing his name. Like everything with Scott, it's impossible to know whether he worked this angle of his overall con as a plotted strategy, or whether he was improvising with the opportunities made possible by the ill-gotten gains generated by the Ponzi scheme. I tend to think he had a definite plan, well thought-out and executed almost to perfection. How else could a working lawyer from the suburbs rise from nowhere to the top of the Fort Lauderdale business, legal, and social scenes in little more than four years from 2002 to 2006?

Consider one infamous night at the National Car Rental Center, where the Eagles were playing to a full-capacity crowd. It has become legend, told and retold by the *Wall Street Journal* and the *Miami Herald,* both of which made it an important entry point for their early coverage of the Rothstein scandal, and it is too good for me to pass up now. In the middle of the concert, Don Henley stood on stage and announced, "I don't normally do this, but this goes out to Scott and Kimmie on their one-year wedding anniversary." People in the audience who knew Rothstein looked at each other and scratched their heads, wondering how Scott pulled that off. For Rothstein, it was simple. He did it with a $100,000 check to one of Henley's environmental charities, the Caddo Lake Institute. The band then launched into its rollicking '70s hit "Life in the Fast Lane," just another one of those sadly hilarious little ironies that abound in the Scott Rothstein story. Rothstein later claimed to Buddy Nevins, a local reporter and blogger, that Henley was merely a friend and no money was involved, but no one believed him. Another story that Rothstein entered into South Florida legend came in 2008 at Governor Charlie Crist's fifty-second birthday party, which doubled as a GOP fundraiser. Party organizers sold the cake's candles for one thousand bucks a piece, but that was not nearly a grand enough gesture for Scott Rothstein. He bought an entire cake's worth of birthday candles at a cost of $52,000.

Similar stories abound. In fact, Scott spent so much money on charitable causes, not to mention personal luxuries (to be discussed later), that the question soon arises of whether Scott's rise and fall, his criminality and chaotic sex life, his supercharged spending sprees, extravagant charitable gestures, and nonstop self-promotion, could be explained by a mental illness or a mood disorder. After all, compulsive spending is a well-known symptom of bipolar disease, one of the most popular diagnoses in contemporary mental health care. As far back as Hervey Cleckley's book *The Mask of Sanity,* psychiatrists have recognized the ability of some disturbed people to mimic normal behavior and fool the people around them for prolonged periods of time. Cleckley called these unfortunates "psychopaths" and devised a list of sixteen characteristics by which a psychopath may be identified. Concepts of psychopathology have, of course, evolved and developed since Cleckley's time, but his pioneering work remains not only fascinating but also surprisingly relevant, in particular with regard to the checklist of sixteen characteristics. Scott can readily be said to embody somewhere between eight and ten of the Cleckley characteristics such as superficial charm and good intelligence or absence of delusions and other signs of irrational thinking, all the way down to untruthfulness and insincerity and an impersonal, trivial, and poorly integrated sex life. Others key points, such as "pathological egocentricity and incapacity for love" are more problematic. Scott was certainly egocentric, but he also truly loved his parents, probably his sister, and maybe his daughter.

While it would be quite handy to label Scott a psychopath and be done with it, a more credible speculative diagnosis might be bipolar disease, in earlier times called manic-depression. As early as 1988, D. Jablow Hershman and Julien Leib identified manic-depression as a trait common among historic high achievers. In their book *The Key to Genius: Manic-Depression and the Creative Life,* they sought to prove that most, if not all, great artists, painters, composers, and writers were fueled by mania and inspired by melancholy. They followed up with an even more troubling volume, *A Brotherhood of Tyrants:*

Manic Depression and Power, in which they examined the careers of three great dictators—Napoleon, Hitler, and Stalin—and found their successes the work of manic, tireless energy and creativity, while their failures look like nothing so much as the paralysis of profound depression. In other words, they embody the characteristics of bipolar disease. In addition to his Ponzi scheme, Scott was well known for his energy, his grandiosity, his charm, his legitimate businesses, his endless partying, and his mistresses and pay-girls. On the other hand, one local executive, who sat at a table next to Rothstein's, observed uncharacteristic behavior at a 2007 charity dinner. The executive rose to introduce himself, but Scott responded with an unconvincing handshake and failed to meet the man's eye in the ninety seconds they exchanged small talk.

"At the time I thought it was rude," recalled the executive, who observed Scott throughout the event. "Our tables were adjacent, but he never gave any energy to those people around him. You could see he didn't give a damn."

The executive, in retrospect, took Scott's behavior as a sign of naked, cynical opportunism. "His sponsorships allowed him to gain credibility in the community and gain status that he didn't have. You're not supposed to steal other people's money to buy tables and sponsorships. I'm sure he was doing all this to build up his law firm, which turned out to be a house of cards."

Of course, it is true that Scott made cynical use of other people's money to project himself as one of South Florida's most important philanthropists, thereby buying his way into social and business credibility. But as a Scott observer myself, I'm not sure that alone accounts for his desultory performance on the night in question. After all, Scott liked to make a good impression at all times. It was much more in Scott's favor, much more supportive of his overall schemes, to be always "on," always the irresistible personality who won over most skeptics with his energy, charm, and humor. The description of Scott relayed by the executive puts me in mind of someone exhibiting signs of depression and flagging manic energy. Could it be that Scott was experiencing the down cycle of a bipolar episode, the reverse of the energy that charged his plans to build a legal and business empire? Perhaps.

Rather than speculate on Scott's moral and psychological state, I asked Dr. Joan Pastor, a nationally respected clinician and industrial psychologist to analyze Rothstein as well as possible from what is known about his behavior from news accounts and interviews—that is, without having the opportunity to actually speak with him. In addition to treating patients at her offices in Beverly Hills and San Diego, California, Dr. Pastor is a highly regarded expert on white-collar crime who consults with major corporations and teaches seminars and workshops to auditors all over the country. Her conclusions are worth considering in some detail. Instead of suggesting a case of bipolar disorder she suggested that he may suffer from a combination of personality disorders.

"You are looking at a situation of someone who fits the criteria for what mental health professionals call a narcissistic personality disorder and an antisocial personality disorder," Dr. Pastor told me. "A layperson would simply refer to someone like this as a narcissist and a psycho/sociopath. A person who is narcissistic is self-absorbed and is focused on getting as much attention, fame, and adulation as possible. Everything is about them and they see themselves as 'special.' Because they are so focused on themselves, they generally do not see others clearly and have a difficult time with empathy.

"The psychopathic personality is considered by most mental health experts to be one of the most dangerous psychological disorders," added Pastor. "This person has little or no regard

Scott and Kim Rothstein examining a new purchase.

for the law and doesn't believe that it applies to him or herself. They want what they want and it can be motivated by anything—power, money, or just to see if they can get away with it.

"It is important to point out that scrupulous mental health professionals are loathe to give these diagnoses, as these disorders are considered very serious ones, and still, I am using these words deliberately because I want the public to understand as clearly as possible this type of behavior," said Pastor. "And even though I have not personally tested Rothstein or interviewed him, he does fit the profile for the hardcore white collar criminal."

Dr. Pastor told me it is important to keep in mind how intelligent Scott Rothstein is. "There is no reason why a deeply troubled person cannot also be very smart and achieve a certain degree of success. However, the challenge is that when you combine the type of mental disorder I've been talking about with a very high intelligence, we are talking

Scott and Kim Rothstein hosting an event in their home.

about a man who is going to want everything possible in life and will do whatever it takes to achieve it." She also suggested Scott may have pressed forward with his crimes, his extravagant lifestyle, his high public profile "just to avoid the monotony that develops when bright people get what they think they wanted and realize it's really not what they want. He could have a perpetual restlessness and a yearning for excitement. Lavish parties, drugs, alcohol, and sexual exploits are not uncommon."

As convincing as Dr. Pastor's insights are today, the pathological side of Scott's character was not apparent during the time he was dominating the South Florida social and philanthropic scene, not even to people who disliked him or found his ostentatious charitable gestures more offensive than helpful.

"Scott had no barometer to tell him that he was way over the top," recalls Richard Rosser, editor of *East Magazine* and a longtime charity volunteer.

Kim and Scott Rothstein at a party.

He kept going like there was no top. Maybe that's where the Ponzi scheme comes in, so he could get more money. He just kept ratcheting it to the next level. It was the Scott persona. Rothstein enjoyed being in the limelight and enjoyed looking the part. I think Scott had this vision that if you look successful people think you don't need money. It's the standard con: the more wealthy you appear, the easier it is for people to give you money. With Rothstein, it was like, you see me giving away money, it means I have a lot of money. That was part of his strategy. Every director in town with all the major charities knew that the checks were coming in from Rothstein and they were being cashed. It was part of Scott's strategy. Anyone can lease a Ferrari, but giving away money is very real.

Not only did this strategy work in terms of building Scott's image and promoting RRA in the legal community as well as attracting investors to the Ponzi scheme, it had the added benefit of demoralizing competitors. One downtown businessman recalls struggling in 2008, trying, like most, to keep costs down and survive what turned out to be the beginnings of the economic downturn. Returning from a charity event, he spotted Scott at a table outside Bova restaurant smoking cigars with some of his regular cronies and generally acting the big shot. "I got home and lamented to my wife, 'Obviously I'm doing something wrong. Here's this guy Rothstein building a company in the worst recession since the Great Depression. I must not be the good businessman I thought I was.' Yeah, it was really frustrating."

David Welch, Rothstein's former neighbor in Plantation and former client in the stolen identity case, remembers Scott's early charitable work at a dinner for the Joe DiMaggio Children's Hospital in 2006, where Rothstein outbid everyone in the silent auction. "It was happening on every single item," Welch said. "He outbid everybody. Scott was putting on a show and it was offensive to many who attended. Scott sponsored events just to get his name out there. His name and the RRA name."

But as Suzanne Migdall, a community leader and charity supporter, remembers, Scott was also very effective, often inspiring or energizing others to imitate his example and give to charitable causes as well. "It was part of his MO," she said. "He was able to pull on our heart strings, the speeches he gave. It's hard for me to talk about him, for a number of reasons. Like many con men, you tend to like him. When you know him personally he's a likable guy. He was always so nice and friendly. He put on a good show."

Andy Cagnetta, president of Transworld Brokers and a member of the board of directors for a number of organizations, including the United Way, concurs. Said Cagnetta, who first met Scott in 2006 at a charity event, "The guy was pretty dynamic. There was a lot of credence to what he was doing. When you first met Scott Rothstein your impression is he is a cartoon character. He's robust, he's larger than life. My first reaction was, 'Who is this guy?' Not someone you'd associate with." But once first impressions receded, Scott often won over skeptics and critics. "He surrounded himself with some very good attorneys," Cagnetta added, "people who were known as the most talented in the legal profession. Then he started giving money to charities. Rothstein became the lead sponsor of several charities I was involved with. Then you say, 'Wow, he came from nothing and he's giving back.' It lowers your radar of someone who I wouldn't associate with. His philanthropy of giving money to major charities was disarming."

Others found Scott's largesse admirable, his personality beguiling. A supporter of the American Heart Association who first met Rothstein before the 2007 Heart Ball remembered Scott as likeable, friendly, and approachable. RRA was the title sponsor of the event, and the supporter attended a 9 a.m. weekday meeting at Scott's house. "When Scott gave his speech as chairman of an event, he always said the same thing. 'We're the ones with the wealth, the fancy cars, expensive watches, and now you need to step up and help the organization. It's my duty and obligation, because of all my success, to give back. Follow my lead, follow my success, and do the same.' Regardless of the charity, it was the same speech over and over." Scott also took care to make his guests feel welcome, offering a tour of the house and showing them his guitar collection and his watch collection before getting down to the business of planning the Heart Ball. "I saw him a few days later at a Humane Society event. Scott was very cordial, inviting me over and introducing me to his friends. He gave me one of his cigars."

As likable as Scott could be, his over-the-top generosity, his need to be the biggest, the first, struck some in the community as obnoxious. When the recession began to take hold in 2008 and RRA just continued to expand, Scott kept giving away unbelievable amounts of money. At the 2009

Boca Raton Concours d'Elegance, which raised more than $1 million for the Boys & Girls Club of Broward County, a live auction included the first model of a new Audi, the R8 V10 5.2 FSI Quattro. The car carried a manufacturer's suggested retail price of about $180,000, but Scott silenced other guests, including Doug Von Allmen, William Scherer, Barry Bekkedam, and Broward Mayor Stacy Ritter, with a bid of $500,000. Audi was so impressed it offered a second car to be auctioned at the event.

But not everyone there was impressed. "Rothstein was decked out in one of his $6,000 suits," said one charity supporter. "He had the chairman's table with the front-row seats, so he was bidding in front of everyone there. I've never seen anyone bid a half-million before—or since. Scott would always arrive the same way, with the same style, and he would always be the top bidder." And yet, he added, the strategy worked. "This was a classic example of a charity event where Rothstein used the Boys & Girls Club to get connected with the ultra-wealthy. And what the Boys & Girls Club did for Scott Rothstein, especially at this event, was to diminish the degree of skepticism surrounding him. Crooks are not usually in the limelight. Rothstein was always front and center with his bling."

Bradford Cohen, a Fort Lauderdale defense attorney with a national reputation, observed Scott's rise and never found it quite credible. Cohen knows what it takes to run a private practice, the discipline, the costs involved, and, like many who gathered at Jackson's Steak House, he was quietly skeptical. "The old guard didn't relish having to deal with him," Cohen said. "To see someone come out of nowhere and in less than two years he's friends with Arnold Schwarzenegger, Hollywood A-listers, Governor Crist. There were always suspicions, and probably a streak of jealousy for many as well."

Cohen, a former contestant on the television show *The*

Apprentice and a frequent expert legal commentator on cable news programs, met Scott at the Capitol Grille early on, when RRA had about ten lawyers on the payroll. He watched as Scott upgraded from a standard Mercedes to a Bentley, a Rolls Royce, and finally a Lamborghini. One week, Scott bought three cars, Cohen recalled, one of which was a Mercedes SLR, a half-million-dollar car. "He said to me, 'I really wanted to get it in yellow, but they didn't have it.' The next week, he traded it in to get the yellow, taking a $50,000 hit. I remember telling my mom, and she said, 'It doesn't make any sense. Even with people who are making money, they don't spend it like that.'"

And yet, while Cohen insists Scott exhibited no competence for business, there was a method to his recklessness: "When you look at any con that's been perpetrated in America," Cohen said,

the con man is cut from the same cloth. The term "money attracts money" is true. They have to put on the façade that they are successful because that's what draws in people. When you have the Sheriff's department which was snookered, it's almost like they were part of the scheme. Scott would say, "I have the Sheriff on my plane," or, "I'm flying with the Chief of Police to a game in New York." Scott was buying legitimacy. To me, people relied on those overt acts to invest with Scott. That was part of his scheme: "Look at me. You should trust me." The stuff you would hear was so outrageous, the way he networked when it came to charity. I remember going to the Bubbles & Bones charity event, and for two years in a row Scott was making crazy donations. Someone would announce, "Who wants to catch a football thrown by Dan Marino? Only fifty grand." Scott would say, "I'll take it!" How can you not be friends with someone who just paid fifty grand to catch a football with you? That's how he got in. People thought he was one of their own. He used those charity events to his benefit.

With Scott, everything was perception. By being seen

Scott and Kim Rothstein at an event.

Scott and Kim Rothstein with a performer.

as a wealthy benefactor giving back to the community, he engendered trust and respect and cultivated new victims for his Ponzi scheme. But he always had to contend with an undercurrent of skepticism and even hostility that ran alongside the admiration, often in the same circles and occasionally in the same individual. There were always grumblings from rival lawyers who could not account for the vast sums Scott spent, donated, and gave to employees.

"Scott was very flashy, the things that Scott talked about were very different from other well-respected attorneys," says one young lawyer Rothstein tried unsuccessfully to recruit to RRA. "He never meshed with old Fort Lauderdale." That's a phrase I've heard over and over again, in interviews with local business people and lawyers. The same was true to some extent about his political influence. True, he was personal friends with Charlie Crist, Florida's attorney general and then governor, hosted fundraisers for John McCain and other Republican candidates, and palled around with national figures such as Arnold Schwarzenegger. He built up a sterling reputation as a Republican Party benefactor and backroom kingmaker, although, as we saw in the Whitney case, he could not even get Governor Crist's Attorney General's office to back off on an investigation of a client. Personal calls from the governor were impressive, surely, but they don't appear to have translated into much real influence. Bernie McCormick, the longtime publisher of *Gold Coast* magazine, wrote a column about a Washington, DC, powerbrokers' event that Scott apparently crashed. It was in honor of George LeMieux, Charlie Crist's longtime top aide and former chief-of-staff, who had just been sworn in as US Senator from Florida.

Rothstein's group, reports McCormick, included Grant Smith, an RRA lawyer and son of former Congressman Larry Smith, as well as political operative Roger Stone, who also worked briefly for or with (depending on who you talk to)

Rothstein, all dressed in ostentatiously expensive suits. The other party involved consisted of staffers and consultants from the administrations of then-governor Crist and past governor Jeb Bush. The latter group was "deeply suspicious" of the first, especially of its leader. "There is a perception that politicians liked and counted on Scott Rothstein for money," wrote McCormick. "The money part was probably true, as few people in Florida wrote bigger political checks than Rothstein, but Republican political staffers were deeply suspicious of Rothstein. Their comments this night included 'things don't add up with that guy,' 'stay away from him,' and 'where is he getting all this money?'" McCormick wrote that Rothstein buttonholed Shane Strum, the newly appointed chief of staff to Gov. Crist, "to make a pitch for one of Rothstein's clients." Strum, however, skillfully deflected Scott's importuning. "If Scott Rothstein was giving the impression to the world that he was best friends with the political elite, the reality was far from that," McCormick wrote.

The impression worked, however, for the seven or eight years of Scott's rise, right up until his crash of November 2009. Indeed, the incident related by McCormick took place only a few weeks before the Ponzi scheme collapsed and Rothstein decamped for Morocco. Suspicions may have abounded, Rothstein may not have gotten what he wanted from Strum, and he may have had to crash the Washington party—but no one dared turn him away, and Strum felt compelled to hold him at arm's length with great care and courtesy. The situation with the business and charitable establishments in South Florida was similar. Many people were suspicious of Rothstein's wealth, and still others were disgusted by his tasteless extravagances and naked need for publicity and attention, but no one turned down his largesse, even as they whispered behind his back. "I was at a Dolphins game," remembered Gary Phillips, Scott's former employer at Phillips Eisinger, "and sitting there I listened to an announcement of an RRA sponsorship, and I thought to myself, 'Do I have to hear this at the football game?' It was more amusing than anything and I just laughed. I got a kick out of watching him buying relationships." And it all worked, the whole magic show, to allay the caution of savvy investors and keep the money flowing into Scott's Ponzi Empire.

My wife, Sandra, and I got a close-up look at Scott's obnoxious need to obtain and manipulate attention at the 2008 Governor's Ball, held at Sun Life Stadium, to benefit the United Way. Most of the guests were dressed in black, formal evening attire, but when Scott made his grand appearance (as usual, with RRA as sponsor) he emerged resplendent in one of his garish $6,000 tailored suits. Sandra remarked that he looked like a Mafioso and wondered if he was celebrating a victory in some big court case. "Well, there's one problem," I replied. "No one ever sees him at the court house, and when I ask other law firms about cases he's handled no one can name any." Why, she wanted to know, did he brandish a big cigar? "I can't tell you," I said. "He's out to impress someone, maybe a lot of people." "I've never seen him in black tie," I said, thinking of all the charity events I'd been to where Scott had flaunted his wealth and bad taste in expensive clothing.

Like many people around town, we speculated idly about Scott, what he could be thinking to dress in that get-up, where his money could be coming from, and whether he actually had the Mafia links his attire and demeanor suggested. Then, Sandra made an astute observation. "Usually, people who are up to no good keep a low profile." I wonder if that was an additional selling point for investors in his Ponzi scheme, those smart money people who should have known better: he was not only slick and charming and clearly making a great deal of money himself, but he were also flaunting it like crazy.

If he were a crook, wouldn't he seek to stay out of the public eye? Brilliant.

As columnist Bernie McCormick noted with his customary clarity, "Rothstein's largesse in the charitable community gave him credibility and opened doors to the wealthy, just as his political donations opened doors to the politically powerful."

It was only a matter of time before the charities Rothstein purported to help would be hit with clawbacks, the government's lingo for paying back the dirty money. Unfortunately, many non-profit organizations were forced to lay off employees or cut services in order to give back money Rothstein had donated. In February 2012, Don Henley's environmental organization announced that it was returning $50,000 of the $100,000 Scott donated that night at the concert to get the Eagles to dedicate "Life in the Fast Lane" to him and Kim. Obviously, this gesture was the result of clawback negotiations with the RRA bankruptcy lawyers seeking to recoup money for defrauded investors. Local charities gave back to Rothstein almost as soon as the Ponzi scheme was exposed, with Holy Cross Hospital, the recipient of $1 million donation, taking the biggest hit.

Chapter 7

Free Spending, Bad Taste

Scott may have developed his Ponzi scheme to attain power and influence as a means to finance some deep, megalomaniac success fantasy. Wealth was a side benefit, but that is not to suggest that he failed to relish the luxuries. For someone like Scott, greed and power can hardly be separated. Money is power, power is money, and in Scott's case, where perception was all, it was something of a chicken-and-egg conundrum—one so strongly connected to the other that we are left to consider which came first. The answer seems to be that Scott cultivated the two gardens together, enabling a sort of cross-pollination between them. The more Scott spent on philanthropy, on building his law firm, and on his personal business empire and toys, the more attractive he became to potential investors.

And how Scott spent! At the time of his rise in 2005, Fort Lauderdale and South Florida were agog at the extravagance—and keep in mind that this is the home of Miami Vice, Madonna, Boca Raton, Dwayne Wade, Palm Beach, and Star Island. Scott managed to stand out in a place already known for its wealth and success. He denied himself nothing, submerging in the freedom to spend money on what he pleased.

Roger Stone, the controversial political consultant who briefly had space in the RRA office, remarked that Scott was "like Rodney Dangerfield at the country club in [the film] *Caddyshack*, throwing money around [and] tipping parking valets $100." At a certain point, the level of spending got obscene, Stone added. "I can see where a person might want one Rolls-Royce. But why would you want two?"

Over the course of the rise, Scott's reputation as a man who spent money inspired admiration, gratitude, subservience, suspicion, and resentment. He was famous for the hand-tailored suits he purchased from Moda Mario on Las Olas Boulevard, each one costing from $6,000 to $10,000. He would buy a dozen at a time, sometimes the same outfit in several colors. These were almost always sartorially cartoonish, intended to evoke a Hollywood image of an Italian mobster. "His favorite color seems to be purple," one associate said. "From the first minute I saw Rothstein, he was like a cartoon villain in a Batman comic book," a waiter at Bova Prime told Bob Norman. "He had these stripes on the Tom James suits and the loud colors. The clothes never fit him right, his body style. He and his wife, Kimberly, would come in and eat, and they would have two bodyguards sitting at a table nearby. Then they would get in a fight and go in different directions, and the bodyguards would scramble around not knowing where to go. I'm telling you, it was comical."

Ron Wise, a former IRS investigator-turned-private consultant, had a similar, if more sober, reaction.

When I first met Scott Rothstein in the summer of 2008, I had been engaged by Rothstein Rosenfeldt Adler to conduct a forensic analysis of documents on behalf of a client. I had expected the lead partner of a major South Florida law firm to convey an image of conservative professionalism. However, the Scott Rothstein I met that morning was very different. Instead of the anticipated gray or navy blue suit, Rothstein wore a plaid sport jacket and a brightly colored tie. He had a gregarious back-slapping demeanor, and he immediately told me his firm could provide me with almost unlimited amounts of consulting work.

Kim's sense of style was little better than Scott's, once she

Kim Rothstein with arms full of shopping bags. (Courtesy Daily Business Review).

gained access to his wealth. She reportedly charged more than $900,000 on an RRA credit card for clothes, shoes, spa treatments, and plastic surgery. The aura of corruption, and in this case I mean fashion corruption, even infected Scott's parents. "I hate to pick on his parents, because they seem like good people, but his father dressed in the most crazy way sometimes," the Bova waiter said. "He would wear these Ed Hardy t-shirts with the rhinestones on them and these baggy, kind of rap-style jeans. I mean, here's a seventy-five-year-old

Scott and Kim Rothstein at Levinson Jewelers.

man in the baggy jeans and an eighty dollar t-shirt. It was comical. All the money, it was just like they won the lotto and didn't know what to do with all the money."

Another local business that benefitted from Scott's free-spending ways was Levinson Jewelers, which he started patronizing back in the early 1990s when both his office and the store were located in Plantation. Rothstein spent millions at Levinson, which opened a grand Las Olas Boulevard store in 2008. His purchases including the $100,000 engagement ring for Kim and a $4,000 Florida Marlins watch he purchased without even seeing it after Robin Levinson, one of the owners, recommended it to him. Scott added it to his growing watch collection. Kim also shopped at the store, spending at least $90,000. It's important to note that Scott and Kim's checks frequently bounced and their credit cards were often declined. Levinson had to dun Rothstein to make good on his purchases—at one point in 2007, she was chasing him for $500,000 in late payments, according to testimony that emerged as bankruptcy attorneys sought to recover Rothstein's

Kim Rothstein and Carole Rome at Levinson Jewelers.

assets on behalf of the victims of the Ponzi scheme. Despite
tardy payments, Levinson Jewelers continued doing business
with Scott. "He was a difficult customer to deal with," Robin
Levinson told the bankruptcy court. "Mark and I made a
decision to sell him jewelry because we always got paid."

Wealth allowed Scott to became a collector, acquiring
impressive collections of objects such as watches (203
timepieces valued at $1 million); guitars; cigars (stacks of
boxes always on hand); vast quantities of sports memorabilia;
an entire warehouse of cars; real estate in Fort Lauderdale,
Miami, Weston, New York, and Rhode Island; and a veritable
fleet of watercrafts. His collection of automobiles included
the aforementioned pair of Rolls-Royces, three Lamborghinis,
four Ferraris (including a vintage model from 1974), various
Mercedes, a vintage 1967 Corvette, a Hummer, a Cadillac
Escalade, a 2009 white Bentley convertible, and the vehicles
most associated with Rothstein's excess: a pair of Bugatti
sports cars (2004 and 2008 models valued at $1.6 million
each). The cars were stored in an air-conditioned building.

One of Scott Rothstein's Bugatti cars. (Courtesy *South Florida Business Journal*)

Scott's boats included the Princess Kimberly, an eighty-seven-foot Warren yacht valued at $5 million; a thirty-three-foot Riva worth $500,000; a fifty-five-foot Sea Ray Sundancer worth around $400,000; and various WaveRunners, Jet Skis, and other personal watercrafts. I can only echo Roger Stone: how many boats can one man sail?

Wealth does not automatically translate to taste. This is especially true of the newly rich, and Scott was no exception. In addition to the clownish suits, which at least served a purpose (to project a persona, as he acknowledged in the 2011 bankruptcy deposition), it is difficult to account for things such as, say, the golden his-and-hers commodes in the $6.45 million waterfront mansion he shared with Kim. As you can imagine, that was only one of the decorating horrors to be found in his house, located on the finger isles of Harbor Beach, a wealthy section at the southern tip of Fort Lauderdale Beach. A contractor who worked on the home sent photos to Bob Norman at *New Times* with these remarks:

The house was over the top gaudy. Lots of golds and deep reds and blue. All the furniture was imported from Italy and a team of folks came from Italy to assemble it on site. He had an indoor theater that had a custom made two-tiered bed upholstered with cheetah print; the walls were covered with hand-carved woodworking. He had a cigar lounge with hand-carved woodworking as well and two seventy-inch plasma screens on robotic arms and four forty-two-inch plasmas on arms.

A retractable flat-screen TV rose out of the bed's footboard in the master bedroom, while the cigar lounge featured "two industrial strength smoke eaters in the ceiling" and a wall of photos of Scott in the company of politicians and celebrities. "It was a shrine to himself not unlike his office. There was an elevator. A massive diesel generator to keep all the audio-visual and computer networking equipment up and running in the event of a power outage. There had to be well over $2 million spent on audio-visual/home automation/networking equipment in the house."

The Harbor Beach mansion was Rothstein's last, biggest house in Fort Lauderdale, just down the street from billionaire Doug Von Allmen's even bigger mansion. Scott's house featured a chandelier that supposedly cost $300,000—I don't doubt it. An amateurish, hand-painted mural adorned the wall of one guest bedroom. A row of interior arches—inexplicable design elements in and of themselves—was also hand painted, this time with ivy. The dining room featured another chandelier, arches canopied in royal blue with golden draperies, and walls more or less the color of Spam. This room, all by itself, looked like a cross between a Golden Age dining salon and a fifteenth century Venetian brothel. The hand-painted ceiling in the master bedroom, with its flowing ribbons and random musical notes, looked like illustrations from a self-published children's book. A downstairs bathroom also boasted a gold

Kim and Scott Rothstein at their Harbor Beach home.

toilet, the contractor reported. "I always took some pleasure out of relieving myself in it," he added.

Riches made everything easier, especially for a man with a haywire moral compass, and doubtlessly removed what few barriers to outlandish, unethical, and illegal behavior might have remained for Rothstein. While Scott's sexual adventurism revolved largely around strippers, escorts and other pay-girls, he also preyed upon the waitresses at Bova Prime, the upscale, downtown eatery he owned with local restaurateur Tony Bova, as well as lawyers at RRA. He was not above using money as an inducement. "Scott was banging all the bartenders at Bova," said one insider. According to public records, he made the following "loans" to Bova bartenders: Sylvie Benioulou, a total of $28,000; Seabrin Kathryn Britt, a total of $20,000; and four loans of $15,000 to Julie Timmerman. In addition, he also lent money to other women, including clerical workers and lawyers at RRA. From public bankruptcy records, it is evident that receptionist Lisa Hirschenson received $5,000, RRA attorney Susan

Dolin got $15,500, and two women whose relation to Scott is not known (at least to me) received $15,000 and $6,000, respectively. I'm not saying all these women were girlfriends or mistresses or pay-girls. Maybe none of them were. But the payments do fit an established pattern. Documented loans, the amounts do not include cash tips, gratuities, or presents. A persistent rumor, for example, claims that Scott gave one Bova bartender a Rolex. Bob Scandiffio, Rothstein's personal bodyguard, said in a *New Times* article, "He did almost every girl at Bova. He spent more time at Bova than he did the office. Everybody knows him, everybody knows how much money he had, and everybody knows how much he spent on the girls. Scott spent so much money on girls that it was ridiculous. I used to get pissed off because they were making more money than I was."

The source of Scott's ready cash was one of the topics at his December 2011 deposition. When Rothstein was asked if he ever kept more than $200,000 in cash at his office he replied, "Sure." Which led to the next deposition question, "What was the highest you ever remember it being?"

"I don't know, a lot, hundreds of thousands of dollars in different places at the office," responded Rothstein. "It depended on what I was doing and how much cash we were taking in . . . I mean, in one fell swoop one day I got $150,000 in . . . Hundreds of thousands of dollars at different points in time in different places within my office. I got a lot of money from organized crime." Scott was not allowed to talk about his connections with organized crime by the Justice Department lawyer present at the deposition, presumably because of an ongoing investigation.

Rothstein then was asked what other sources provided him with cash. "I used to get cash from my restaurant," he responded. "I used to go down there and get cash when I needed cash. I got money from—I got cash from certain

Scott Rothstein and a friend having a good time at Bova Prime.

friends and clients that were paying me to then pass the money onto people who were going to do things for us."

His responses not only piqued the attention of the questioning attorney Sam Rabin, but also that of the other three dozen lawyers sitting in on the deposition. Rabin then asked what the money was financing, what types of crimes. "Money laundering, extortion, physical violence," Rothstein replied. "Public corruption, influencing law enforcement, influencing bankers, influencing businessmen, influencing business owners." Judging from the Justice Department's alacrity at preventing Rothstein from testifying further on matters such as these mysterious references, I can only assume that many, many additional indictments are yet to rock Broward County. Unless, of course, this is some elaborate ruse, some complicated, long game being played by Scott.

Straddling the divide between work and play, between collecting expensive toys and real business investments, is Rothstein's interest in real estate. Scott's lust for acquiring property seems to have preceeded the Ponzi scheme. As far back as 2003, well before the Ponzi scheme geared up (but, remember, not before Scott was already cheating clients), he pulled together a $1.2 million loan to buy his first eastside home, a waterfront house on Castilla Isle, one of the prestigious finger isles that splay off from Las Olas Boulevard as it approaches the Intracoastal Bridge and the beach beyond. Thereafter, the real estate spree got underway in earnest.

Of course, as the Ponzi money rolled in, this little micro-empire was not nearly enough to satisfy Scott, who told himself and others that his real estate acquisitions were investments, not compulsive buys or a hoard. Not even the unbelievably garish $6.4 million Harbor Beach mansion, already described in some detail, satisfied him—Scott also owned a vacant lot across the street priced at $1.8 million; a high-rise, two-bedroom Manhattan condo at One Beacon Court (also known as the Bloomberg Building) that he bought for $5.95 million in 2008; and a $2.8 million home in Narragansett, Rhode Island. Rothstein invested in less ostentatious properties, too, including a $715,000 condo in Lauderdale-by-the-Sea, four miles north of Fort Lauderdale Beach on A1A; a fifty-five-hundred square-foot executive home in Plantation worth almost $1 million; a $260,000 Plantation condo where Cheryl Lynn Shaffer lived; a $475,000 Weston condo turned over to Debra Villegas; a $435,700 condo at Las Olas Place used for trysts with escorts; and other residential and commercial properties throughout Broward County. There is also evidence that Scott invested in two Brooklyn buildings with the controversial builder Dominic Tonacchio, once touted as the centerpiece of a revived Fourth Avenue. Tonacchio was an investor in Scott's Ponzi scheme, receiving payouts totaling $2.6 million through October 2009. If the loss of Scott as an investor caused the Brooklyn development's financial shortfalls, as some New Yorkers allege, then his is another community damaged by Scott's dishonesty.

Among Scott's fantasies was the one that portrayed him as a savvy businessman, a Trump-style wheeler-dealer with a finger in every pie from luxury watches to cruise lines to high-end vodka, and for a time the Ponzi money allowed him to play this charade with gusto. Some people were fooled, although it's not always easy to determine who actually saw through Scott's posturing and who was merely trying to cover their embarrassment after he was unmasked as a con man. Take Roger Stone, Richard Nixon's one-time campaign advisor and the consultant generally credited with founding the modern, dirty-tricks era of political campaigning. The late Lee Atwater, author of the Willie Horton gambit that doomed Michael Dukakis and ensured the first Bush presidency in 1988, also gets tapped with the title, but Stone predates him by almost two decades. In fact, Atwater was a Stone protégé. By 2003, Stone was no longer living not quite so high on the hog when he landed in Fort Lauderdale, where Scott Rothstein, then acquiring shady operators for his firm and business the way a chess player acquires pieces, snapped him up. Scott gave Stone office space in the law firm, the two of them founding something called RRA Consulting. The idea was that Stone would provide public affairs consultations for RRA's legal clients, which would fit in nicely with Scott's vision of RRA as a one-stop law firm. But RRA Consulting never managed to attract a single client. "Having spent time with Rothstein," Stone later wrote on a blog, "I am at a loss to understand why a serious investor would give huge sums of money to a venture he created. Rothstein had no prior business success, no business acumen nor track record that would engender confidence in an investor. He could not read a balance sheet. He could not write or read a business plan. Rothstein was a lawyer, not an entrepreneur."

"Stating the obvious," Stone added, "Rothstein always seemed to me to be more interested in the 'appearance' of success and influence rather than the reality of either." Looking back, it can be amusing to observe Scott playing pretend business mogul, buying up businesses or parts of businesses like a little girl playing tea party. He invested $7 million in an Internet technology company called Qtask, a California company that claims its secure server guarantees the privacy of client companies and their communications.

"Scott used to say Qtask was our retirement plan," said Stuart Rosenfeldt. "He said it was going to be as big as Amazon or Facebook or any of the large Internet success stories. Everyone was raving about Qtask." Rosenfeldt characterizes Qtask as "a project management software" brought to Scott's attention by Rob Bushell, who did some work for the company, and Russ Adler, who became fascinated by it. "They thought it was going to be the end all and change all for the judicial system," Rosenfeldt said. "Scott was a strong believer in Qtask and told me we owned a third of the company. I subsequently found out that I didn't own anything with Qtask, which is good."

RRA used Qtask for certain sensitive emails among key lawyers and others at the firm. Scott bought a thirty percent interest in Renato Watches, the luxury watch company owned by his pal, Ovadia Levy, son of alleged Israeli mobster Shimon Levy, and Daniel Minkowitz. Scott started out collecting Renato watches, then befriended Levy, and then bought into the company. I can imagine Rothstein thinking, "Hey, I really like these shiny things—I think I'll buy the company!" It seems obvious to me that Scott viewed both these investments as sexy businesses that might eventually provide a return. A central part of his business plans seems to have been to throw as much stuff against the wall as possible in hopes that some of it would stick and provide a big score, and if it didn't, at least the sexy investments burnished his public persona as a bold and savvy businessman. Actually, though, Scott seems to have been loath to conduct ordinary due diligence before sinking money into a business or a property. In part, this is the result of his restless, impetuous nature, which contributed to a belief that normal rules did not apply to him and which always sought a short cut, and in part, it was driven by the need to put some of the ocean of Ponzi money to work somewhere, somehow. Scott also seems to have bought into companies only to lose interest.

Sometimes things worked out best for Scott when he neglected his side businesses. Take Jewel River Cruises, the abortive European cruise line he partnered with veteran industry executive and close friend Albert Peter. It was supposed to be a "boutique" cruise operation offering all-suite cruises of European rivers, somewhat similar to the ultra-lux voyages offered by Silversea Cruises, a Monaco-based company that sails six all-suite ships to exotic destinations all over the world. Silversea maintains a Fort Lauderdale operation, where Rothstein served as the company's local attorney, which is how he became such good pals with Peter, then the Silversea CEO. That arrangement soured, however, when Rothstein and Peter allegedly conspired to blackmail Silversea's owner, the wealthy Italian businessman Manfredi Lefebvre d'Ovidio. According to *New Times,* Peter was dissatisfied with his compensation package and concocted the harebrained scheme with Scott, who doubtless thought he could con d'Ovidio as easily and profitably as he had Doug Von Allmen or Ed Morse. The plan involved one of Rothstein's cronies imitating a federal maritime official and another (reportedly the versatile Steve Caputi) pretending to be a reporter. I can only imagine the excitement of these associates at the chance to stretch beyond their usual acting roles as bank executives verifying nonexistent trust accounts.

When Peter and Rothstein flew to Monaco to put the bite on d'Ovidio, however, they found themselves overmatched.

Not only did the blackmail scheme fall, d'Ovidio fired Peter and sent the pair of miscreants back to Fort Lauderdale, tails between their legs. That's when they cooked up Jewel River Cruises, which was supposed to be a Swiss-based company, although Peter's office was always in borrowed RRA space in Fort Lauderdale. Jewel River Cruises, facing one delay after another, never sailed a maiden voyage. Peter unceremoniously vacated his RRA office six months before Scott's Ponzi Empire crashed. The friendship with Rothstein was not a total loss for Albert, however. According to suits filed by bankruptcy trustees, he invested $2.1 million in the Ponzi scheme, earning a $1.5 million profit, plus another $400,000 in salary, not to mention the $4.3 million Scott paid to keep Jewel River Cruises afloat, all of which came out of the Ponzi scheme proceeds.

Some of Scott's dozens of companies existed only to make campaign donations to Rothstein's favorite politicians. For example, the only function of TLKRJ, LLC, owned jointly by Scott and Boca Raton restaurateur Tony Bova, seems to have been to pump $200,000 into the campaigns of candidates running against Scott Israel for Broward County Sheriff. This race eventually was won by Al Lamberti, the incumbent appointed by Rothstein pal Governor Charlie Crist. "All of a sudden, we had a guy named Bova from Boca dropping all this money on the race, and no one knew why," Israel told Jose Lambiet of the *Palm Beach Post.* "Then we figured out Rothstein was involved and that they wanted Lamberti to win." Yet Rothstein hedged his political bets in that race, funneling $160,000 into Democrat Israel's campaign via donations made RRA attorneys, which infuriated Roger Stone, the old GOP warrior. Stone broke his association with Rothstein and their political consulting firm when Scott threw his support behind Democrat Alex Sink in the 2009 governor's race, won by the Republican candidate, Rick Scott.

Indeed, the partnerships between Bova and Rothstein were

in some ways both the most significant of all Scott's business ventures and the most puzzling. "Tony was a very successful restaurant owner in his own right," said Tom Prakas, a hospitality-business broker. "I don't know why he needed Scott Rothstein." But that view discounts the charisma, energy, charm, and aura of wealth that Scott brought, almost at will. At the time of Scott's fall, Miami businessman Rodney Barreto, serving as chair of the 2010 Super Bowl host committee, was planning to invite Rothstein to join the committee and bring with him sponsors and referrals. "He was a force, don't kid yourself," Barreto said. We've already seen how Scott was attracted to the hospitality industry, for complicated reasons, through his legal representation of strip clubs. One of his earliest entertainment clients and longest and most loyal friends was Steve Caputi. The two men met in the mid-1990s when Scott was a young employment lawyer in partnership with Howard Kusnick and represented Iguana Cantina when it was registered as a Florida corporation in 1996. Over time, as Rothstein began to earn significant money, he invested in Café Iguana, a trendy twenty-one-plus nightclub in Pembroke Pines, and Caputi eventually became tightly wound into Scott's Ponzi scheme and other machinations.

Owning part of a nightclub wasn't enough for a man like Scott, who had seen for himself the importance of an upscale restaurant where Fort Lauderdale's power elite gathered. After all, he had largely started his climb to prominence and success at Jackson's Steakhouse and continued it at the Capital Grille. He wanted a place like that at the heart of his burgeoning empire. He set his sights on Riley McDermott's, an upscale restaurant on the ground floor of the Bank of America building on Las Olas Boulevard, the same building where Rothstein Rosenfeldt Adler had its offices. Riley McDermott's was owned and operated by Anthony McDermott, a self-style "Southie" from Boston who had made a $25 million fortune when he sold an Internet company he had founded and developed. Later, McDermott claimed to reporter Bob Norman that he never had liked or trusted Scott Rothstein, rebuffing numerous entreaties to invest in the Ponzi scheme. Scott attempted to cultivate McDermott by inviting him to the RRA skybox at Dolphins Stadium for a football game along with some of the regular Rothstein crowd, including Ted Morse and George Levin. McDermott said he also declined offers to invest in Qtask. "They were looking to raise capital, and I looked at their platform," he said. "We looked at it and saw that you could already get what they offered elsewhere, from Microsoft. They had a good team who really believed in it, but we weren't interested."

But if Scott couldn't get his hands on McDermott's millions, he was happy to settle for the restaurant. First he managed to persuade McDermott to hire RRA as the restaurant's lawyers, with Christina Kitterman handling the account. Then RRA's lawyers made Riley McDermott's their primary gathering place—a logical development, if only for the sake of convenience. The lawyers, Scott included, no longer had to leave the building for lunch or dinner or all the alcohol they needed to relax or have a good time. Like Robin Levinson, though, McDermott found that Scott disliked paying his bills. Unlike Levinson, he seldom actually got paid. Indeed, for all his posturing, McDermott appears to have been outwitted by Rothstein at every turn. He claims Scott stiffed him on a $100,000 bar bill, including $20,000 for the wake of Melissa Britt Lewis, the tragically murdered RRA partner. "Of course, I didn't want to talk to him about it at the time. I didn't feel it was appropriate, you know, the girl had just died," he said. "I said, 'I'll talk to Scott later.' Not once did they offer to pay that bill."

When Scott finally offered to buy the restaurant for $3 million, McDermott claims he was almost relieved. He was tired of RRA lawyers coming in everyday and "drooling"

Kim Rothstein, Scott Rothstein, Laurie Bova, and Tony Bova at Bova Prime.

over the waitresses and bartenders. He was tired of comping Scott's police friends from around Broward County and the platoons of off-duty police officers Rothstein hired as security. And, most of all, he was tired of nagging Scott to pay his bar tab, always receiving the same response: "I'm working on it." Yet McDermott also claims that after Scott wired $2.5 million to pay for the restaurant, he never came up with the remaining half-million dollars, which means he bought the restaurant at a discount of almost seventeen percent, and that's not even counting the alleged outstanding bar tab. In any event, Rothstein got what he wanted, a primo restaurant space in the same building as his law firm. He partnered with Tony Bova to reopen the place as Bova Prime, and it quickly gained a reputation for exorbitant prices, excellent food, and the natural habitat of beautiful women and wealthy and powerful men. It debuted near the apex of Scott's four-year run as a force in the South Florida legal, business, and charity scenes. The quick, nasty slide was just about to begin.

Chapter 8

A Penumbra of Violence

Scott Rothstein took possession of Riley McDermott's restaurants in September 2008 and held a grand opening for Bova Prime restaurant the following January. Kim was in attendance, along with the up-and-coming actor Adrian Grenier, star of the HBO show *Entourage,* who performed with his band, the Honey Brothers. During its brief lifespan, Bova Prime became the trendiest upscale eatery in downtown Fort Lauderdale, even though the *Sun Sentinel*'s restaurant reviewer, Judith Stocks, rated it only two stars. The joint was "stunningly designed," Stocks wrote, but that only raised high expectations that food and service failed to meet. The food was "average tasting and disappointingly served lukewarm," while "having to ask for ice refills on a slow night doesn't belong in the same room with a bill that easily tops $200 for two." And this poor performance came four months after the restaurant opened, when kinks in the operation should have been long since ironed out.

No matter. Bova Prime was the place to see and be seen, and it was packed nightly by the wealthy, those who wanted to appear wealthy, and those who wanted to be next to the wealthy. Sports and showbiz celebrities were not uncommon sights. In addition to local pro-athletes who frequented the restaurant, such as Ronnie Brown and Channing Crowder, so did performers such as the rapper Ludacris. As Kevin Gale wrote in the *South Florida Business Journal,* Bova immediately became the premier power lunch spot in Fort Lauderdale.

Tony Bova and Scott Rothstein at Bova Prime.

The *Miami Herald,* reporting on the official opening, marveled at "a menu of still and sparkling waters, including a $40 bottle of Bling H20," as well as "celeb sightings," and a private champagne room with "a mere $1,000 minimum. Powerbrokers cut deals over imported Japanese kobe."

It was also a place where Scott's fantasy of wealth, power, and machismo, fueled by alcohol and the ubiquity of beautiful young women, became contagious. You never knew when bluster might escalate to blows, when bodyguards might draw guns, and when the Fort Lauderdale police might arrive to separate rich posturing men with more ego than maturity, more testosterone then sense. That no one ever got bloodied, let alone shot, only added snickering comedy to the mild yet dramatic sense of danger. It was kind of like being on an adult Disneyworld ride.

Bova had not been in operation long when a drunken Anthony McDermott showed up on St. Patrick's Day, nursing resentments and looking for trouble. "For an Irish kid from Southie," he later boasted to Bob Norman, "that's a good

Kim and Scott Rothstein at a social Bova Prime evening.

way to get into a brawl." After all, at the beginning of the previous summer this had still been his restaurant. He had sunk $4 million into renovations and named it after his seventeen-year-old son. In addition, Rothstein still owed him a large sum of money, both for the restaurant itself and for the food and drink. Among the regulars at Bova, of course, were Scott, his friends, and his associates, which led Rothstein Rosenfeldt Adler attorneys to call the pricey restaurant, with a combination of mockery and proprietorship, "the company cafeteria." McDermott says he told the general manager to bring him two whiskeys and Scott Rothstein. His plan: ask Scott for the money. "I knew his answer was going to be 'I'm working on it, I'm working on it.' So I was going to send him to Broward General with a broken jaw."

Joe Alu, a retired Plantation police officer serving as Kim's personal bodyguard, remembers the altercation differently, though with no less macho bravado. McDermott came into the restaurant drunk and unruly more than once, said Alu, one time claiming the computers were his, another that he wanted the steak knives. In the first instance, Alu and Christina Kitterman calmed McDermott by showing him the paperwork conveying the computers and other items to Rothstein in the sale of the restaurant. On the other occasion, Scott instructed Alu to give McDermott the steak knives just so he would go away. Alu protested, insisting McDermott had no right to the knives, but Rothstein was firm. On the night in dispute, however, McDermott strode into Bova, talking angrily about how Scott had "stole" his place, Alu said.

"McDermott was running around the restaurant, yelling 'I can't believe this k--- Jew stole my f------ restaurant," said Alu, who called the police. Even McDermott, according to Norman, admitted saying to Rothstein, "You're a lying, fat, f------ Jew. You're a thief and a liar, and you are pillaging this community." Later, he insisted he didn't mean to use the word "Jew" as "a racist remark. I was just telling him to get his head straight because he was a disgrace to this religion."

The incident came very close to real violence. McDermott claimed he gave Rothstein "a shoulder fake" to make him flinch, while Alu said that McDermott "clenched his fist and jumped at Scott." Alu put his hand on his gun, McDermott claimed. According to Alu, he grabbed McDermott by the throat and "slammed his head into the window a couple of times." Police arrived at the playground—I mean restaurant— separated the posturing men, and made no arrests. Alu denied a rumor that he and other bodyguards "beat up" McDermott. "If I beat him up, you wouldn't see him around," Alu boasted. "He would be in the gutter." Tough talk, especially when, on the day Scott was sentenced, he got into a pushing match with local TV reporter Jack Hambrick, who was attempting to stick a microphone in Kim Rothstein's face. Alu, who is built like a bodybuilder and carries himself like an aging motorcycle outlaw, shouldered Hambrick and pushed him away. Hambrick, who is fit but slender, like a tennis player or a swimmer, pushed back—driving Alu into the bushes and onto his back. Not the finest moment for a beefed-up former cop, getting physically overmatched by a mere reporter.

Whichever version of what happened that night at Bova is closest to the truth—Alu's or McDermott's—no one comes out looking very responsible. But both illustrate the toxic contagion of the fantasy Scott was busy casting around himself, like a wish-fulfillment magic spell. Scott glamorized himself as smarter, more manly, and more competent than anyone else in the room, able to move seamlessly from one world to another—from court to boardroom to political backroom to charity banquet hall to strip joints or social clubs where Mafia deals are done, men are made, and hits are sanctioned.

In another Bova incident, guns were actually drawn. On a day before Scott took over the restaurant from McDermott, he stationed a "spotter" named Robert Heider in the place to make sure employees didn't steal anything in advance of the ownership transition. A personal enemy of Heider's, a man named Robert Handler, stormed into the restaurant

A friend, Scott Rothstein, and Tony Bova at Bova Prime.

A friend, Kim Rothstein, Scott Rothstein, and Tony Bova at Bova Prime.

bent on an armed confrontation. Rothstein bodyguards
Robert Scandiffio and Jose Morales were called down to the
restaurant. Morales got into a loud argument in which he
allegedly relieved Handler of his Glock pistol. An FBI agent
eating at the restaurant witnessed the ruckus and called
police, who arrested Handler on a firearms charge, while
letting the other men go free. This anecdote, a prologue to
Scott's imposition on the restaurant, proves that his reputation
preceded him. I don't know how close anyone came to pulling
a trigger—Scandiffio was also armed, though he did not draw
his weapon—but once a gun appears, anything can happen.
And somehow, I don't think other restaurants experience
many incidents like this one, not even in Broward County,
where, traditionally, organized crime has owned a stake in
many eateries, the better to launder ill-gotten profits.

The question becomes just how much of Scott's chosen
image of a Mafia-connected tough guy is sheer fantasy and
how much of it is real. Many have speculated that Scott
could not have originated and maintained the Ponzi scheme

on his own but must have had the backing of some criminal mastermind, perhaps someone he met at one of the strip clubs he both represented and frequented. Maybe he met a don through Steve Caputi, his partner in Café Iguana, who proved a loyal friend and valuable asset in perpetrating the Ponzi scheme. The image was useful for more than merely boosting Scott's ego. Some very smart people in the community bought into it "hook, line and sinker," as *Sun Sentinel* columnist Michael Mayo wrote in a piece defending an earlier story published when Rothstein was riding high, in which he called Scott by the Yiddish term "macher." As Mayo explained, "That means big shot. With a persona that's part Joe Pesci wise guy, part H. Wayne Huizenga entrepreneur, and part Imelda Marcos spender, Rothstein, forty-six, has roared from relative obscurity to the top of the local power structure in astonishing time."

Scott must have savored a special little thrill when he read that "Joe Pesci" line, after he had worked so hard, with the expensive suits, the larger-than-life tipping at bars and clubs, the tough-guy bravado, and the boasting about his Mafia uncle beating people on a rooftop in Brooklyn.

The one clear-cut instance of direct interaction with the American Mafia and the Italian, curiously enough, comes in the aftermath of his downfall, but I don't want to get ahead of myself. Scott did do business with one notorious and powerful organized-crime figure, though the business in question, as far as I can determine, had more to do with both legitimate business and gulling investors into the Ponzi scheme than it did with the kinds of things that mobsters traditionally earn from their riches, such as extortion, prostitution, drugs, loan sharking, bookmaking, and so forth. One of Scott's closest friends, Ovadia Levy, is the son of Shimon Levy, who could be said to be a multi-millionaire hotelier but who can also be said to be an Israeli mobster, or at least to have ties to the Israeli mafia. Levy has been linked to the list of eleven top Israeli mobsters that scandalized the Jewish nation when newspapers first reported its existence in 1977. In 1981, Levy spent a year in an Israeli prison for hiding a crime kingpin wanted for two grisly murders. Immediately after his release from jail, Levy immigrated to the United States, settling in Broward County where his holdings include the Sea Club Resort on Fort Lauderdale Beach. According to the *Miami Herald,* he was granted a visa to enter the United States only because immigration officials didn't know of his Israeli conviction as an accessory to murder until after the fact. Levy's criminal record in Israel reportedly also included convictions on charges of tax evasion, insulting a police officer, giving false testimony to a police officer, and "suborning perjury by urging a police officer not to prosecute an acquaintance."

Shimon Levy has been linked to other alleged Israeli organized crime figures, such as Eli Tisona, currently serving a nineteen-year sentence after being convicted on charges of laundering $42 million through Miami jewelry stores for the Cali cocaine cartel. Tisona was convicted even though two potential witnesses were murdered just before the trial. Levy lived in a Plantation home once owned by Shalom Genish, a well-connected businessman who owned the largest construction firm in Israel until he had to flee charges of bribery and tax evasion. Arrested in the Bahamas on a fake passport, Genish evaded prosecution by offering to testify against an alleged hit man in a federal case targeting an Israeli money-laundering ring in Nassau. To further suggest the influence of Israeli organized crime, Levy's criminal record was ordered destroyed in 1989 by Chaim Herzog, president of Israel, but those records somehow emerged in a later civil suit against Levy in New Jersey, which is how we know about his colorful past today.

In 1997, Shimon Levy's minority partner and manager at Sea Club Resort, Zvika Yuz, showed up for work one morning, only to be shot in the face as he parked his car. His assailant, as seen by several witnesses, was described as a man sporting a "fake beard and carrying a doll," "who walked unhurriedly to a waiting vehicle and drove away." Shimon Levy told the *Miami Herald,* "I knew him for three years very well, and I don't see any reason for something like this. He's not a guy that deals with illegal stuff. He's a very straight guy. He's a good husband. He's a good father." That may be true, but Yuz was also involved in one of Florida's biggest Ponzi schemes (until Scott came along, that is), the Premium Sales con that defrauded investors of between $300 and $500 million from 1989 to 1993. Thirty-five people were charged in that case, a grocery wholesale scheme similar to the $880 million Ponzi fraud perpetrated by Nevin Shapiro in Miami in 2010.

Yuz was not a principle in the Premium Sales deals and avoided prosecution, but he did funnel $22 million into it, mostly from rich Israeli investors, including Shalom Genish. In the time surrounding Yuz's shooting, two other men associated with Premium Sales were murdered. Isaac Benarroch, an investor who had lost $600,000 in the deal and made personal threats against Yuz, was found shot in a Georgia hotel where he was on a tennis vacation. Ricardo La Bergere, a Venezuelan businessman associated with Benarroch, was shot outside his son's apartment building in West Palm Beach by a man wearing a motorcycle helmet. No one was ever arrested in any of the three murder cases.

Shimon Levy, according to the *Sun Sentinel,* invested $28,145,000 in Rothstein's Ponzi scheme, while Ovadia Levy invested $12,551,100. Many people have assumed Rothstein and Ovadia Levy became friends because of Scott's interest as a collector of luxury watches. After acquiring several Renato models, he bought one-third interest in the company, as we've noted earlier, becoming Ovadia's business partner. But Stuart Rosenfeldt told me that Scott and Levy first met and became friends at the Downtown Jewish Center Chabad in Fort Lauderdale, the temple where both men and their families worshipped. Scott was ostentatious (though apparently sincere) in his religious observance—until his downfall, the Chabad's main building bore the name The Rothstein Family Downtown Jewish Center Chabad in honor of a multi-million-dollar donation made by Scott. But even here, in the matter of faith, Scott sought the edge. He allied himself not with the legitimate Hasidic Orthodox house of worship, known as Chabad Lubavitch of Fort Lauderdale, but with a breakaway institution founded by a charismatic rabbi, Schneur Kaplan. When Kaplan first came to South Florida in the late 1990s, he worked within the Lubavitch hierarchy with Rabbi Moishe Meir Lipszyc, who reported to Rabbi Abraham Korf, director of the Lubavitch Education Center in Miami Beach, who in turn answered to the Lubavitch World Headquarters in New York. After founding his own renegade congregation, Kaplan answered to no one.

Rabbi Korf, the Miami-based regional director of the 145 affiliated Chabads in Florida, said Kaplan was "removed" from the Chabad hierarchy because "he does not follow the rules and regulations that Chabad stands for." Korf declined to go into detail, but said Kaplan was warned "many times, but it didn't help . . . It's not right for me to tell what he did. We have our own system. We don't do things in public." He added that "if everyone did what they want, not act by the regulations, there would be no more Chabad."

A disillusioned former Chabad "insider" who spoke to Bob Norman said that Kaplan broke with the Chabad hierarchy at about the same time he met Scott. The rabbi "set out on his own and did what he had to do. In other words, he put his interests first." The insider said that Kaplan "comes across as this charming, charismatic man who is otherwise unassuming and doesn't make judgments. But I'll tell you now, he's the f------ Jim Bakker of Judaism." No one knows precisely how much Scott gave to the Chabad, but the insider said it was between "three to five million," though admittedly that's an educated guess. The actual number is bound to be big. Big was Scott's style, and it was certainly big enough to get his name on the building. Unlike other charitable recipients of Rothstein largesse, however, Kaplan and the Chabad may be able to dodge efforts by the bankruptcy trustee to claw back some or all of the money Scott donated. The Chabad, citing "clergy privilege," is resisting trustee attempts to gain information about Scott's donations. "The privilege protects Kaplan from being rolled up in the Rothstein case and it prevents the government from seizing the building," said the insider.

If the Chabad is a cult, as the insider alleges, then Scott seems to have indulged in the Kool-Aid. "Rothstein once told Kaplan he was going to buy him a house," the insider said. "Rothstein said he loved Kaplan. Rothstein never refused the rabbi a dollar, and when the rabbi needed money, he went to Rothstein." At the dedication of the new building, the insider said, "Scott gave a little speech where he talked about how walking with the rabbi was like he was a little boy again and walking with his grandfather. Then he said, 'I go down on bended knee for you people. I salute you.' And there he is on his knee in his $10,000 suit. It was great theater and total b-------."

The insider said he doubts the truth will ever come out about whether the money Scott gave the Chabad came from the Ponzi scheme. And who else made major donations to the Chabad building? Scott's friend and business partner, Ovadia Levy.

Like Rabbi Kaplan, Ovadia Levy is keen to keep the bankruptcy trustees' hands off of his principle enterprise, Renato Watches. In October 2010, long after Scott had gone to jail, Levy and his partner Daniel Minkowitz filed a petition with US District Judge James Cohn urging "caution" in order to "preserve their interest in and ownership of seventy percent of the stock of Renato." In other words, they argued that Scott's partial ownership of the company was not significant enough to make it fair game for seizure by the bankruptcy court. So far, that argument has prevailed.

Apart from Renato and the millions that Levy invested in Scott's Ponzi scheme, his ties to Rothstein include charitable and political donations that appear to have been coordinated. Levy joined Scott in donating $15,000 each to the John McCain presidential campaign in 2008. Both have been major supporters of the American Heart Association—in fact, after Scott's fall, Levy continued his participation, becoming a "signature sponsor" of the Broward Heart Ball in 2010. Both men drove Bugattis worth $1.5 million. Both men hired off-duty police officers as bodyguards. No one has ever really explained what was going on when Levy called the Plantation Police Department for personal protection on the very day that Rothstein missed his payment scheduled to investors shortly before he fled to Morocco. Levy's explanation was met with universal skepticism. He asked for a uniformed police officer to stand guard outside his home from midnight to 5 a.m., he said, because he was worried that "suspicious teens" might vandalize his high-end automobiles, including, in addition to the Bugatti, two Lamborghinis and a Rolls-Royce. Levy's request was approved, and he received police protection outside his home for three weeks beginning Oct. 26, 2009, at a cost of $32 per hour, or $3,582 total. As Bob Norman noted in his blog, Levy lived in Hawk's Landing, a suburban, gated, luxury community with twenty-four-hour security. It remains to be discovered why he would need additional police presence in the wee hours of the morning.

"The timing is suspicious, to say the least," observed

Norman in his blog, openly skeptical of the "suspicious teens" explanation. "Levy didn't mention the massive crime that was beginning to unfold when he contacted police." Norman did not spell out the implications, but he clearly assumed Ovadia Levy knew about the Ponzi scheme at a time when no one else did, if the Ponzi scheme is the "massive crime" he alluded to here. Did Levy feel the need for special protection because of some degree of involvement in Scott's fraud? Some in Fort Lauderdale have speculated that Scott must have had help from organized crime to concoct and carry out a con as complicated as his Ponzi scheme. Was it Shimon Levy? Perhaps, as Norman implies, Ovadia Levy was nervous some other investor might take offense at the huge payments Scott Rothstein wired to Ovadia Levy, Shimon Levy, and other members of the Levy family in early November 2009. In the month preceding his downfall, Scott plundered the trust accounts at TD Bank, sending $232 million "into a dizzying maze of businesses," including $15 million wired to Morocco, presumably to finance his life in fugitive exile. Some of that fortune, though, Scott spent out in payments, among them nearly $3 million to Ovadia Levy, Shimon Levy, and other members of the Levy family.

Scott forwarded these payments to one Levy or another as he flew to Morocco in a chartered jet, which suggests that he considered his situation a matter of urgency. Bankruptcy trustee William Scherer expressed curiosity about the payments. "I don't know why [Rothstein] would be paying some investors and not other investors," said Scherer. "And it doesn't matter because money paid within ninety days goes back to the bankruptcy court as a preference. So they aren't going to be able to keep the money." But Scherer noted one exception to that rule: "I am concerned some of that money may have gone to the Mob," said Scherer. "And the thing about the Mob is they don't give money back."

And of course, a Mob connection would explain why Scott feverishly sent payments from the plane taking him to exile in North Africa: fear. Morocco may have had no extradition treaty with the United States or Israel, but organized crime by definition does not recognize international law. I can't help but imagine Scott in the air, frantically punching in the numbers to wire money to Levy, thinking about the prospect of opening the door to his luxury apartment in Casablanca one day, sooner or later, and finding a man in a fake beard, carrying a doll, waiting in the corridor.

Chapter 9

Beginning of the End

The way Scott Rothstein made use of police officers to give the appearance of personal security was, of course, much more extravagant than that of his friend Ovadia Levy. The law enforcement presence around Scott; his wife, Kim; their home; and his restaurant quickly became one of the most noted emblems of his personal and professional excess. Whereas Levy hired Plantation Police to watch his house in the early hours of the morning for three weeks, Scott had twenty-four/seven police protection for seven months until the Ponzi scandal broke and the Fort Lauderdale Police Department, embarrassed, halted the practice on November 2, 2009.

During that period, off-duty, uniformed officers accompanied Scott and Kim to public events, guarded Bova Prime and the offices of RRA, and kept a round-the-clock vigil at Scott's Harbor Beach mansion. The cost totaled $1,080 per day ($394,200 per year) and was paid in its entirety by Scott to the police officers, not to the city. As in most cities, it is customary for off-duty police to work as private security, most often in stores or nightclubs. It is not unusual for there to be more off-duty police working the streets than those on duty—a good thing, as off-duty cops can readily assist active-duty officers if the need arises. Yet the arrangement Scott forged with the police department was unprecedented.

Rothstein pointed to the March 2008 murder of RRA partner Melissa Britt Lewis as justification for spending so much on police protection. "You can call me extra-security conscious," he said, "but at the end of the day, no one close to me is going to be killed, raped, attacked, harmed in any way so long as I have the ability to provide extra protection. I am a businessman. I don't want to be followed home and shot." But former Rothstein business associate Roger Stone expressed the feelings of many in town when he called the police presence "part of a carefully constructed image designed to convey power and influence." In the immediate aftermath of Lewis's killing, Rothstein hired private bodyguards. It was after a year that he added off-duty cops. Whatever else his motivation, a uniformed police officer gave Scott a higher profile than a suited bodyguard.

The murder of Melissa Britt Lewis, known as "Missy" to friends and family, remains one of the most puzzling aspects of the Scott Rothstein story. She left RRA for a time, by some accounts from shame over her old relationship with Scott, but returned to become partner not long before she was killed. At the time of her death, she was thirty-nine years old, an attractive woman, still young, ambitious, well-liked, and with a reputation of honesty and integrity. The day after her murder, as news of her death spread, people were shocked all along the downtown business corridor. A friend who knew Lewis from a class sponsored by Leadership Broward, a non-profit organization that provides leadership-skill seminars to corporate executives, told me that day, "One of my Leadership classmates has been murdered, I just saw Melissa a couple of days ago and I still can't believe it." Just hearing the reactions of her friends and associates left me with an eerie feeling. It seemed unreal that an up-and-coming attorney became a murder victim. At five-foot-three, Lewis dressed well and carried herself with authority. She had honey-blond hair and a ready smile. Her ambition was to become a judge.

Much of the speculation about the murder revolves around Melissa Britt Lewis's perceived honesty versus

Scott's elaborate swindles. Fueled by the lack of information released by police, a rare occurrence in a state with one of the best open-records laws in the country, many people think—or perhaps would like to think—that Lewis was murdered because she somehow learned of Scott's Ponzi scheme or of some of the tactics Scott employed to support it, such as the shenanigans at TD Bank. Had she known, her friends and associates agree, Lewis would certainly have gone to the authorities. Perhaps Scott, or someone in his employ, arranged her untimely end, said the whisperers. Or perhaps it was one of Scott's shadowy supposed partners, the Mob men. In this scenario, Melissa was murdered to keep her quiet. Or maybe Scott, rather than hiring someone to murder Lewis, manipulated the anger, fear, and prejudice of a mentally unstable man, nudging or taunting him into killing Lewis.

This last theory implies virtually superhuman powers of evil, knowledge, and persuasion on Scott's part. I have to admit, as I've researched Rothstein's life and crimes, it has fired my imagination and exerted a powerful gravitational pull on my mind. The prospect of Scott like some fat Iago in a law office working on a weak personality such as that of Tony Villegas can be almost overwhelmingly seductive. Something in the heart wants to believe. In the end, though, this theory is the bogus allure of the super villain or the conspiracy theory. Scott was exceedingly smart, and by most accounts a good lawyer, and incredibly charismatic and charming when he put forth the effort. But he was not the Joker, or Goldfinger, or Professor Moriarty. The Tony Villegas-as-a-puppet-of-evil idea, with Scott as the puppet master, is just too far-fetched to be supported.

Still, many questions about the murder remain. Lewis was first reported missing by co-workers when she failed to arrive for work at RRA on March 6, 2008. Police went to her home in Plantation, a well-established suburb west of Fort Lauderdale with wide streets and large Florida-style ranch houses, where they found signs of a struggle in the garage. Her black Cadillac SUV was missing. Investigators quickly determined that Lewis had been seen the previous evening shopping at the nearby Publix supermarket on Broward Boulevard, leading to speculation someone had followed her home, although it seemed more likely her assailant was waiting for her to arrive. Within a few hours, police recovered her car, abandoned in the parking lot of a medical office building a mile away. As the *Sun Sentinel* reported at the time, it appeared Lewis had "put up a fight, given the amount of pepper spray" in the car. Bloodstains were found in the trunk, along with her shoes and a woman's brown suit jacket. There were also pepper spray stains on the walls, floor, and ceiling of the garage. The following morning, Friday, March 7, her body was found, fully clothed, floating in a canal not far away. Lewis had been beaten around the head and neck and strangled. She bore bruising and cuts on her arms, indicating she put up a ferocious struggle for her life.

The investigation soon focused on Tony Villegas, who was suspected of being jealous of the relationship between Lewis and his estranged wife, Debra. They confided everything to each other, with Debra helping Lewis get over her heartbreak when her husband of five years asked for a divorce. Melissa had been encouraging Debra during her separation from Tony. Both women had survived difficult childhoods, though Debra's was by far the worst of the two. "I grew up very hard in rural Texas, and my parents were not very good parents," Debra told Plantation police detectives. "[Melissa] was the only person in my whole life who has actually loved me and been good to me." By contrast, Tony Villegas was a controlling and abusive husband and father who once told Debra that if she ever tried to leave him, he would feed her to the alligators so she couldn't be found. Debra also said Tony enjoyed watching violent movies and once talked about "crossing the line," by which she took him to mean he could kill somebody. "He's just crazy," she told police. "He's just nuts, you know."

Melissa practiced employment law, a legal specialty that drew many lawyers to represent the wealthy corporations that were most often the defendants in such cases. But though she became a lawyer in part because she enjoyed "the finer things in life," said her aunt, Lynn Haberl, she worked "as the defender of the underdog." She represented the ordinary people who thought their employers in some way had exploited them. "If she felt that someone had been wronged," said longtime friend Tonja Haddad, "she would basically be in your corner and fight you to the end." Family and friends knew Melissa as a gourmet cook who spent money lavishly on her sister's children. She loved Disney World. "She was the aunt everybody would wish they had," her former attorney colleague said. "She made everyone feel good."

After Villegas moved out, Melissa began spending so much time at Debra's house that Aimee, Debra's grown daughter from a previous marriage, told police, "I always joke, 'Yep, Melissa's our dad. She does our groceries; she takes care of us; she spoils us at Christmastime; she spoils my son. We go to the Keys together. She makes sure we have everything that we need." Aimee credited Melissa for helping Debra find the courage to kick Tony out after an abusive rage in which he smacked his son in the head with a schoolbook and shoved Aimee, who was pregnant at the time, out of the way when she tried to intervene. "She's my mom's backbone," she said. "My mom, without Melissa, she wouldn't have ever left [Tony]."

The two women were sufficiently concerned about Tony Villegas and his perceived capacity for violence that Melissa bought pepper spray, and Debra bought a Taser. Melissa sent an email to fellow lawyers in December 2007, asking advice on making a will. She wanted to protect Debra's children in case Tony acted out. "My friend Debra is going through a divorce," she wrote. "Her ex-husband is nuts. To be on the safe side, she wants to be sure she designates who gets her children if he hurts her and goes to jail. Seems extreme, but you have NO IDEA what is going on and restraining orders are worthless." According to testimony given police by Caleb Villegas, Tony's son, Villegas blamed Melissa for the end of his marriage. Picking up Caleb and his brother for the weekend, Villegas once noticed Melissa's car parked outside the house. "He's like, 'The reason we probably got a divorce [was] so they can spend more time together,'" Caleb told Plantation police. "'Cause she had gotten a divorce. Melissa got a divorce from her husband at the same time as my mom and dad got a divorce. So he thought it was planned for a while, like they were planning to get a divorce at the same time."

After Melissa's body was found in the canal, the police investigation, guided by the alleged history of violence related by Debra and her children, quickly devolved upon one suspect: Tony Villegas. He was arrested within a week, the day after a memorial service for Lewis. In the early weeks and even months that followed, the evidence against Villegas was perceived to be shaky, at least in the press and by those members of the community who gravitate to message boards and the comments sections of Internet news stories. Apparently, Debra originally told police that while Villegas had been abusive toward her, he had no problems with Lewis. His jealousy, she said, was aimed at other men, potential rivals. "Debra Villegas on Sunday said Tony Villegas and Lewis were always cordial and that she did not sense that he harbored ill will toward the woman the couple's children considered an aunt," according to the *Sun Sentinel*.

By the next day, however, Debra was saying the exact opposite. *The Miami Herald* reported she alleged her estranged husband murdered her best friend out of jealousy over how close they were. "If a dog showed me attention, he'd be jealous of it," she told the *Herald*. "He was jealous of her, and in turn killed her because of it." I have not been able to persuade Debra Villegas to consent to an interview for this book, nor have I seen an explanation elsewhere for why she changed her perception of Tony's view toward Melissa so drastically over such a short period of time. Reporter Bob Norman certainly found it curious, and mentioned it prominently in an early analysis of the case in which he called the evidence against Villegas "scant," "muddled," and "insubstantial." He also lambasted the Plantation Police Department and the State Attorney's office for sealing the arrest affidavit in apparent violation of the Sunshine Law. "In Florida, you're supposed to tell the people why you've locked one of their fellow citizens in a locked cell," Norman wrote. "Police spokesman Phil Toman and prosecutor Howard Scheinberg argue that probable cause for the arrest can't be made public because the investigation is 'fluid' and 'very active' at the moment. Well, maybe they should have waited until they had a case before they arrested Tony Villegas for the murder." Norman cited the sealed affidavit and weasel-worded pronouncements by authorities as further indication of the weakness of the case against Villegas.

After Villegas's arrest, his family and friends expressed astonishment and skepticism. His mother, Aida Villegas, said her son was a decent man trying to adjust to divorce. "He's been a very caring guy, a very hardworking guy. A family man. A good son," she said. He was a family man who had changed his shift so he could be home during the day and care for the children while Debra was working at RRA. He cooked the family meals. A childhood friend, Luis Castineiras, told reporters that Tony Villegas "is not a violent person." One of Villegas's attorneys asserted his innocence. "He really is completely bewildered by the whole experience," said Michael D. Walsh. "He knows who Melissa Lewis is, but he doesn't know her. He doesn't know her house. He doesn't have a beef with Ms. Lewis." At Villegas's arraignment, his family and his lawyers asserted that he was being framed. "There was absolutely no reason whatsoever for Mr. Villegas to kill Ms. Lewis," said Walsh. "Zero."

Tony Villegas has not yet gone on trial for the charge of strangling Melissa Britt Lewis to death in her garage with his bare hands. A judge found him unfit to assist in his own defense and sent him to a mental hospital after experts testified he was depressed, refused to take his medication, and broke down in tears whenever asked about his family or the charge against him. "He appeared lethargic, unmotivated to assist himself," testified one psychologist at the May 2010 competency hearing. "He can't elaborate, has difficulty clarifying." Villegas complained to doctors that his anti-depressant medication made him feel bad, but evidently he resumed some kind of treatment while in the hospital. In April 2011, a judged deemed him able to assist in his defense and therefore competent to stand trial. The trial has been delayed several times, and at the time of this writing, has not been rescheduled.

After the Scott Rothstein Ponzi scheme was exposed in November 2009, speculation that Tony Villegas was a fall guy, framed for the murder of Melissa Britt Lewis, flamed up higher than ever. In comment sections and message boards, suspicion centered on Scott Rothstein, who was seen as a criminal mastermind of the order of Kaiser Soze. Villegas's attorneys, of course, seized upon the controversy. Pointing out that Villegas had no prior criminal history, they announced that they wanted to depose Rothstein. "The extraordinary recent developments have opened up whole new avenues to explore," co-counsel Milian told the *Sun Sentinel*. "There are too many coincidences. It's huge, an incredible set of circumstances." Lead defense counsel Bruce Fleisher was even more forceful: "The unfolding Rothstein saga sheds light on the power and intimate connections Scott Rothstein had with law enforcement and government. We have to take another look at this." It implies, as least to my mind, a theory much loved by the message board conspiracy theorists, many of whom believe that the Plantation police helped their fabulously wealthy, former union attorney get away with the murder of an innocent young woman and the framing of an innocent (if unstable) man. Joe Alu, who later became Scott's primary bodyguard, was a former Plantation cop, while Howard Scheinberg, the original prosecutor on the case, eventually went to work as a lawyer at RRA. Some observers see conflict of interest in these developments.

The rest of the theory goes something like this: Melissa Britt Lewis was a smart, tough lawyer of the highest ethical standards who learned Scott's fraudulent and illegal activities from her friend, Debra. As chief operating officer for RAA, Debra knew as much about Scott Rothstein's business as anyone except for Scott himself. If she was not privy to the naked truth about the Ponzi scheme, she certainly knew that bad, unlawful things were going on. Some theorists believe that Scott did the killing himself. They point to Lewis's house—the burglar alarm undisturbed, her dogs safely inside—as evidence that the killer was someone she knew and trusted and who probably accompanied her home from the grocery store. One variation has Scott hiring someone, possibly a former Plantation police officer, to kill Lewis and frame Villegas.

Like most conspiracy theories, any of these notions may be intriguing to propose, but they strike me as extravagantly improbable. Each one violates Occam's razor, the philosophic principle that asserts that the most concrete explanation should be developed until abstract elements are proved necessary. For one thing, these theories are complicated and lend Scott almost supernatural powers of cunning and malice.

He was smart, but he probably wasn't this smart. He was selfish, self-centered, and indifferent to the welfare of others, even those close to him. At the same time, he valued loyalty in others, and I'm sure he was able to congratulate himself on those conquests wherever convenient, as with longtime loyal associates such as Debra Villegas or Melissa Britt Lewis or, for that matter, Stuart Rosenfeldt. In the end, Scott's villainy caused all of these people pain and suffering to one degree or another, but in his egomania, I am sure he thought he could keep everything under control, right up until the moment that his machinations flew apart in all directions.

In the immediate aftermath of the murder, Scott and RRA put up a reward of $250,000, and Scott was in the gallery every time Tony Villegas appeared in court, right up until the day he fled to Morocco. "We'd go to a status conference and he'd be sitting there up front, glaring at us," said Milian. "I thought it was unusual that he'd take such an interest." Milian obviously intends to make Scott's attendance look suspicious if not villainous. But does it really seem like the behavior of a man who arranged the murder of one of his closest associates? To me, these are the actions of a grieving friend. "There is an absolute, crazy lunatic out there," Scott told reporters in the days between Melissa's murder and the arrest of Tony Villegas. "Anyone that would hurt this woman is really a complete lost person, very dangerous." However hollow these words and gestures may seem in light of Scott's later fall, I see no reason to believe he was not sincere at the time. But still—anything is possible with Scott.

The evidence against Villegas did not turn out to be quite so flimsy after all. In a long analysis by reporter Lisa Rab that appeared in *New Times* in April 2010, Tony Villegas's history of emotional instability and domestic violence was reported in detail for the first time. It leaves the impression of Villegas as a controlling, insecure, and erratic personality, and few readers will come away thinking he's incapable of killing

Melissa in some kind of delusional fugue. I am not saying he's guilty—it is prudent to avoid reaching conclusions of a suspect's guilt or innocence based on news stories, even well-reported ones. At this point, I am not privy to evidence of guilt or innocence that may be presented to a jury, so I try to withhold judgment, even in the privacy of my own mind. But the theory that Villegas murdered Melissa Britt Lewis is more credible to me now that it was earlier in the investigation.

Police have never recovered Melissa's missing iPhone, but it remained on for a couple of days after her death. By tracking the cell tower hits—a smart phone "pings" nearby towers on a regular basis, even when not in use—they were able to track its path of travel during that period. The record shows that the phone traveled west from Plantation to I75, then south until it stopped moving in Hialeah, the city in neighboring Miami-Dade County where Tony Villegas lives. Villegas's phone "pinged" the same Hialeah cell tower as Melissa's. The next morning, according to court documents, "The victim's cellular telephone tower hits closely mirror movement and times for the suspect's departure, path, and arrival to work. The records also mirror the delay until Villegas' train leaves the FEC train depot as well as the suspect's known path and times of travel during his work day of March 6, 2008."

When police first questioned Villegas, he broke down in tears, telling investigators that the idea that Debra was dating other men and taking them to the home he had shared with her made him upset. "I don't like flies on my meat, if you know what I mean," he said. He denied personally knowing Melissa Britt Lewis. Questioned about pepper spray, Villegas insisted he had never come in contact with it. His landlord and roommate, Wilset Pascual, however, told investigators that he saw Villegas attempting to wash pepper spray from his arms at about 11 p.m. on the night of Lewis's murder. Villegas asked him if he knew how to remove pepper spray, saying he'd gotten it on him when he was moving some boxes and a canister went off. Police also found a Google search about pepper spray on the records of Lewis's iPhone.

The most explicit evidence, however, was found in the trunk of Melissa Britt Lewis's abandoned Cadillac SUV, in the form of that brown suit jacket. It was the same jacket she was seen wearing at RRA on her last day of work. Police say Tony Villegas's DNA was found on it, presumably a hair or possibly skin cells, deposited there during the struggle that left pepper spray stains in Lewis's garage and which ended with her being throttled to death at the hands of a physically powerful man. To date, police have refused to identify the nature of the DNA evidence, but as Lewis was not sexually assaulted, it could not have been semen.

The evidence against Villegas certainly seems sufficient to warrant arrest and trial. The question of his guilt I'll leave up to the jury. Time remains for new developments, with Rothstein scheduled for another deposition and another two dozen bankruptcy trials on the horizon. Combined with what we know about Scott and his reaction to Lewis's murder, the evidence against Villegas points strongly away from any theory that implicates Rothstein in the death of Melissa Britt Lewis.

By contrast, her killing marks the critical turning point in the career of Scott Rothstein, master of an empire built on lies and fraud. At the time, Scott seemed to be riding high—acquiring businesses, houses, and cars; making breathtaking contributions to charities; influencing political campaigns; and attracting much of Fort Lauderdale's top legal talent to RRA—but it was in fact the beginning of the end. Scott was badly shaken by Melissa's murder. He began spending big money on personal security and bodyguards. He paid less attention to business and more to girlfriends and toys. He developed a tic. His ADD got markedly more noticeable.

Less than eighteen months later, it was all over. Two years later, Scott Rothstein was behind bars.

Chapter 10

Decline and Fall

Scott Rothstein and his Ponzi scheme might have flourished for years before the inevitable crash, if only he had paid more attention to his business. Bernie Madoff, for example, kept his funds rolling for a decade and a half, from 1992 to 2008, while Brooklyn investment manager Philip Barry bilked small investors in what was the longest (and possibly the shabbiest) Ponzi scheme ever, barely keeping afloat for thirty years beginning in 1978. By contrast, Scott was a comet blazing out over downtown Fort Lauderdale in less than five years. Why? It is not a question of whether Scott was a smart operator. Part of the answer lies in the fact that Scott became too caught up in the trappings of wealth. He appears to have been especially diverted by the several girlfriends he kept on the side. In addition, he paid too much attention to the legitimate companies he began acquiring and took too little care of his core business, the Ponzi scheme. His decline and crash can also be attributed to the mounting pressure that Scott felt in the eighteen months following the murder of Melissa Britt Lewis.

By any measure, 2008 was a glory year for Scott: the pinnacle of his power, wealth, and influence. On January 26, he married Kim at Casa Casuarina, the Versace mansion in South Beach, with Governor Charlie Crist and his then-fiancé, Carole Rome, in attendance. At a reported cost of $1 million, the wedding was the culmination of a three-day bacchanal at the mansion. Scott enjoyed it all so much that he bought an interest in the property, which included a hotel, restaurant, nightclub, and private membership club, with his company, the Bova Group, assuming management responsibilities. Scott continued to recruit South Florida's best and most high-profile lawyers to RRA, including former prosecutors and judges, namely past Boca Raton mayor Steve Abrams and former judges Julio Gonzalez, William Berger, and Barry Stone, building up the firm to seventy attorneys. He did this by paying exorbitant salaries that were subsidized by the Ponzi scheme. Reportedly, RRA's payroll was $18 million, although it billed legal fees of only $8 million. Of course, no one knew this at the time. People wondered where the money came from, but no one thought Scott was an out-and-out con man.

Stephanie Toothaker, then a rising legal talent at Blosser & Sayfie, first met Scott at Jackson Steakhouse, where she and other members of the firm would go for a drink after work. "Scott was there," she recalled, "living large." Soon, Scott began aggressively recruiting her to join RRA. "Scott

Scott Rothstein in front of computers and phone at his desk in his Rothstein Rosenfeldt Adler office.

gave me a tour of the office, showed me all the different things, where Roger Stone's office was," Toothaker said. When they finally sat down to discuss the offer, however, she found it "an extremely disjointed conversation." Scott had three computer screens and he constantly checked them. He frequently interrupted negotiations to answer the phone. She found it impossible to have a continuous conversation—until he asked her point blank what it would take to bring her to RRA as a partner. "How much are you willing to pay me?" she asked. Scott replied, "$400,000." "You don't need to see my book, my list of clients, for conflict checks?" Scott replied, "Nah, we don't need any of that. We just want you."

When Toothaker said she would have to bring two associates with her, Scott answered, "No problem. We could pay each of them $150,000." After some chitchat, much of it about the University of Florida, where both Scott and Stephanie did their undergraduate studies, she left.

> I remember walking out of his office thinking, "$400,000 is a high salary. If you don't have the book to show that you can support that salary, how can he offer it?" My perception was that he had some very good attorneys that worked there. I started doing the math in my head, what attorneys were being paid, and what their books probably were. It didn't seem to support a traditional law firm model. How did he bring over these attorneys? It didn't really make sense to me, not that I don't think I'm worth every dime of that salary.

Toothaker also thought it was "weird" that RRA lawyers didn't fill out time sheets. "I know for a fact the attorneys were not filling out time sheets," she said. "So how do you bill your clients?" Suspicious of where the money was coming from, Toothaker and her associates decided not to join RRA. "At our firm, the partners would joke about where their money came from," she said. "As time passed, and [RRA] continued to add high-quality lawyers, we'd say maybe they are legitimate. Maybe they've figured out something the rest of us haven't." This was in the early months of the 2008 economic downturn, when every other law firm in town was struggling, but RRA kept adding attorneys at ever-higher salaries. "Scott was throwing money at club memberships, political events, and they were doing it at a time when every other law firm was making cuts," Toothaker recalled.

Other lawyers around town found RRA's success frustrating. RRA lawyers were known to have coffee and breakfast in the morning from ten o'clock to eleven o'clock, lunch from noon to two o'clock, and by three o'clock be having drinks at Bova. One former judge at the firm was rumored to spend his days reading the newspaper. "As a legal community, we saw how well their attorneys were living," Toothaker recalled. "We would go to meetings such as the County Commission, where we would have a client. And RRA had no one there. Where were their big clients who are paying big fees? We wondered what we were doing wrong."

Toothaker and the rest of the legal community found RRA's success baffling. "To me it seemed like they were not really running a law firm," she said. Most observers assumed Scott was making money with nontraditional clients. She knew the rumors that Scott was involved in the pornography industry, Internet gambling, and/or some kind of money laundering. Scott once made a remark to Toothaker about a client having something to do with the Internet who was under FBI investigation. Everyone knew Scott relished representing strip clubs and other traditionally shady businesses, and everyone in the business community could see he affected the look of a cartoon Mafia member.

Somehow, all of this posturing and image-mongering worked for Rothstein. Looking back, it is hard to imagine that the high-powered lawyers he attracted to RRA over the last few years of his heyday were not put on guard by his behavior as Toothaker was. If you were one of the most successful, known, and respected lawyers in town, or a former judge or mayor, and you were working for a firm that has a lead partner who pays the highest salaries in South Florida, how would you take seriously a lead partner given to clownish antics who opens his company-wide emails with the salutation "Hey kidzzz!" and closes with "Love ya"? Somehow, this kind of rank unprofessionalism raised no misgivings in the minds of the overpaid, elite legal talent working at RRA in 2008 and 2009. No doubt, they thought they were worth it. Getting an ego stroke and a big paycheck can go a long way toward soothing an otherwise wary and skeptical spirit.

In any event, Scott Rothstein was flying high at the peak of his profits—sometimes literally. He flew by chartered jet to sporting events in New York, political get-togethers in Tallahassee, and anywhere else that struck his fancy. In 2008, he flew to New York so often that he paid $5.95 million for a two-bedroom luxury condominium in midtown Manhattan. He used the jet to schmooze with political operatives, too. According to Roger Stone, that summer Scott flew a group of friends, including Stuart Rosenfeldt, to the Republican National Convention in Minneapolis, where his pal Charlie Crist was on John McCain's vice-presidential short list. Also on board was Shane Strum, a top staffer for the governor who later became Crist's chief of staff. Rothstein reportedly took advantage of the occasion to lobby Strum in behalf of RRA's participation in an anticipated class action lawsuit against the pharmaceutical industry. The earlier, more famous class action against the tobacco companies earned some lawyers a contingency fee equal to $112,000 per hour. That is serious money, even by Scott's standards, and he wanted a piece.

According to Roger Stone, who was also on board, Rothstein argued that rather than having the attorney general litigate the case in-house, it should be given to RRA on a contingency basis. Scott argued that his firm already had contacts in other states that were likely to take up similar class action suits against drug makers. Rothstein's pitch failed. "It never went anywhere because McCollum doesn't like [contingency work]," said Stone, who despises Scott today and has no good words for him. "He was largely politically inept," Stone said. "Rothstein lacked understanding of who's in control. You don't go to the governor to get the attorney general to do something. But Rothstein likes to go to the top, to take the fast track." Remember, Stone also blasted Scott's abilities as a businessman. It is impossible to reconcile, even as more time passes, Stone's portrayal of Rothstein as an all-around incompetent, when the image many in Fort Lauderdale have of him is that of a master manipulator.

The truth no doubt lies somewhere along the spectrum, in between hapless bungler and evil genius. It may have been a sliding scale, depending on how distracted Scott was at any given moment. But there can be no doubt that, in 2008, Scott was rolling in money, women, influence, cigars, watches, vodka, cars—everything that his inflated ego desired. He may not have achieved his goals all of time—for example, he did not convince Shrum to acquiesce—but he did have a top aide to the governor of Florida flying on his jet. He had access.

I have no doubt that Rothstein possesses a brilliant mind and a powerful personal charisma that enabled him to influence men and women alike. How else can someone explain his ability to fool and defraud clever and wealthy businessmen, such as Doug Von Allmen or Ed Morse? Charlie Crist really was among his best friends, and it was not entirely based on the campaign contributions that Scott lavished on the governor. People saw something in Scott. And yet, Scott's

Scott Rothstein swaying a crowd at an event.

wiles let him down in a relatively short period of time. Like many egomaniacs, he began to believe his press and the stories he was putting out about himself. As he wrote in the mitigation letter he prepared for Judge Cohn, he developed an "insatiable desire to have a law firm that would be the envy of others." However, he openly admitted that "I had neither the client base, nor the financial resources, nor the requisite skill set to do what I set out to do. . . . But I would not accept failure. . . . I became 'the master' self-promoter, lying about everything from the size of the firm to its successes. I began to live a life both personally and professionally that my business could not support."

The problem with liars, especially highly successful ones, is their propensity for believing their own untruths. Scott began to think he really was just as talented, powerful, and masterful as he pretended to be. He lost any understanding that his high life could ever end. He began to think that he deserved the praise, the perks, the cars, the houses, the companies. He deserved to drink during business hours; to carouse with friends, marks, and minions every night; to spend time with his six regular girlfriends and the half dozen other women he was chasing. Eventually, it all took a toll. It was too much drinking, too much entertaining, too much womanizing. He failed to give the Ponzi scheme the attention it demanded. Scott, though smart and a gifted attorney, did not really want to practice law. He wanted to be like one of those partners in his ex-wife's law firm, the ones he described to Gary Phillips as making $2 million per year without working hard.

At RRA, Scott was able to live that fantasy of a legal executive mastermind, building a large firm with international reach (offices in Fort Lauderdale, Boca Raton, West Palm Beach, Tallahassee, New York, and Venezuela), which he could manipulate without having to exert too much effort.

One thing that Rothstein did not know about Ponzi schemes, however, is that they are hard work, and the longer they run, the harder they are to manage. The schemer must cultivate a constant influx of new investors so that their money can be used to pay off earlier investors and finance the appearance of wealth and success to lure in even more. If Scott had kept his eye on the ball, he could have made some corrections that would have prolonged the lifespan of the scheme for several more years.

Not only was Scott aware of the rumors about him, he courted attention in every way: with his ostentatious lifestyle, through his exorbitant spending on charities and political events, and in select interviews he gave to local reporters. In October 2008, he entertained questions in his office from Bob Norman of the *New Times*. "Who is this guy?" Norman asked rhetorically. "Is he for real, or is he building a house of cards?" Today, the answer to those questions range from a sad shake of the head to a clenched jaw to helpless laughter, but at the time Norman still treated Rothstein with no more than friendly skepticism. Rothstein, for his part, knew how to give a whiff of red meat to an always hungry reporter. Sitting behind his desk in his opulent sixteenth-story office, surrounded by his showy photos and three computer screens, Scott said, "This is where the evil happens." Acknowledging the perception that he rose too fast and spent too much, he said, "Look, I sleep in the bed I make. I tend toward the flashy side, but it's a persona. It's just a f------ persona."

Norman, still getting to know Rothstein, described him as "friendly and funny, even gregarious," but also "mercurial and aggressive." Rothstein warned that everything written about him had better be correct, slipping in a bit of a Bronx accent to spice the implied threat. Later, he confided "the stresses of being Scott Rothstein." A standard question that people asked Rothstein was how he found the time to sleep.

He said, "I'll sleep when I'm dead. I'm a true Gemini. I joke around that there are forty-three people living in my head and you never know what you're going to get." Norman then asked how Rothstein arrived at that number. "I counted them one day. There are some philanthropists in there, some good lawyers, and I like to think some businessmen. There are also some guys from the streets of the Bronx that stay hidden away until I need them. Does that sound crazy? I am crazy, but crazy in a good way."

We can only imagine what those pressures were. By this time, there is no doubt that Scott was dancing as fast as he could, soliciting new investors to keep the Ponzi scheme going. On top of that, he was busy donating money to charities, buying real estate, investing in an array of businesses, and living large both out of a growing taste for the crasser perks of wealth and to keep up the image of a high-powered, highly successful Fort Lauderdale wheeler-dealer. "Failure was not an option," Scott wrote in his mitigation letter to Judge Cohn. "Word had already spread like wildfire about RRA: the firm to watch, the firm to beat, the newest power player. I was determined to do whatever I had to do to make it work, which was simply to continue a charade that was, in hindsight, clearly doomed to fail." In one of his greatest understatements, Scott admitted, "I had completely lost my moral compass."

Despite the lies, Scott believed that he could have pulled out of the scheme and paid everyone off if he had stopped early enough. Because there were no actual loans or pre-settlement investments, Scott personally guaranteed investors' money, manufacturing a fake TD Bank website to show potential investors that he had the collateral to pay them back in the event that things went badly. "I always had every intention of repaying the money," Scott wrote. "I had exit strategies to pay everyone off and move forward. And in the early part of this horrific scheme, I could have pulled out of the spin, paid everyone off, and lived a beautiful life." All he had to do was reel in his spending, slow the firm's growth, "and most importantly, reel in my ego. But that would have required me to admit that the persona I had created for myself and the world, the successful lawyer, entrepreneur and businessman, were not superhuman. That I was fallible and had, in fact, failed. And my greed and ego were not going to allow that to happen."

Scott's greed and lack of caution made him a tempting target to an equally sharp operator, according to a $37.6 million bankruptcy clawback suit filed against RRA general counsel David Boden. It occurred in the failed Jewel River Cruises business Scott attempted to launch with Albert Peter, former CEO of Silversea Cruises. After Peter became partners in Jewel River Cruises, Scott paid him $403,000 in salary, plus an additional $400,000 to Peter's wife for "unknown reasons," according to the $8.7 million clawback suit filed against Peter in October 2010. The two men forged a deep bond, regularly socializing with their families and counseling each other on personal matters—none of which prevented Peter from stealing all of the funds that Rothstein and Boden had sent overseas for the benefit of Jewel River Cruises, a sum that Bob Norman figures at $4.3 million. According to the clawback suit against Boden, the entire Jewel River enterprise was a scam to defraud them after Peter somehow figured out that Scott's riches were stolen. "Rothstein and Boden did absolutely nothing about Peter's con," the clawback suit alleged, "because they knew they could not either sue for or report the theft of money to authorities that was already stolen." Trustees believe that Peter is living somewhere in Switzerland, no doubt in ill-gotten luxury, and expect to serve him with papers soon.

Imagine what a blow it must have been for Scott to be

betrayed and outwitted by one of his closest friends. It is essentially the same con that Scott pulled on many of his own friends as well as people he didn't know. By early 2009, the strain on Scott was starting to show. People around Rothstein noticed it, including Ms. North Beach. A beautiful young businesswoman, perhaps Scott's longest and most important girlfriend, reported that Scott "had more ADD. His attention span faded. It was terrible. He was pulled in so many different directions. It was not the normal Scott that I knew. His twitching got worse." Many people around town noticed Scott's pronounced twitch. "He would sit and talk to me and his head would twitch," Ms. North Beach said.

Ms. North Beach first met Scott in 2006, after he was already involved with Kim No. 2 but well before the infamous Versace-mansion wedding. She provided many insights into Scott's character and his development. Like everyone else in South Florida, she suspected Scott was up to something, but she had no clue it would turn out to be a Ponzi scheme. "My suspicions were the Mafia," she said. "Definitely the Mafia, when I heard about his past and where he grew up in the Bronx, that whole persona. He had a tough side to him that not many people knew. He talked about his sister, who had gotten beaten up, and how he went over there and kicked the guy's ass. He went to jail for it, he told me that, too. To me, he acted more Italian than Jewish."

Although she wasn't aware of the Ponzi scheme at the time, Miss North Beach knew Scott intimately over most of the rise and fall of his criminal empire. The bond between them was not primarily sexual. "[Sex] was okay," she recalled. "It wasn't that exciting. We didn't have that kind of connection. We had an intimate connection, but it was more than that, and he knew it, too."

What drew her to Scott was his personality. "He was alive. He was fun," she said. "Scott was a child because of the way he acted and held himself. He would do just anything. He had no fear." The first night she slept with him at the house he shared with Kim, he showed her his boat, his dog, and his refrigerator full of wine and sat down at the piano, where they sang together. "It was amazing," she said. "His voice was very high and I have a back-up singer's voice. We sounded beautiful together." Scott told her that Kim was out because she had been using too much cocaine, presumably a reference to rehab, though I can find no other evidence or reference to support this—it may have been a lie of seduction.

When Ms. North Beach came downstairs the next morning, she found Scott praying. "It kind of opened my eyes. When we were talking, he was passionate about praying, which he does every morning. We kissed goodbye and I drove [home]. I began talking with him periodically."

Apparently, Scott trusted Ms. North Beach—he certainly seems to have let his guard down with her. He told her that Kim liked threesomes. "Scott said they always used to be with other women," she said. "Those were his exact words. 'Kim likes other women.'" Kim didn't mind Scott's other girlfriends, but she felt "threatened" by Ms. North Beach, and called to tell her to leave Scott alone. Photos of Scott and Kim as the happy, young, power couple are not sincere, she said. "I remember him saying he needed to give Kim something to do to get her out his hair. Then he said he was making her director of real estate." Kim, she said, used to leave a plate of Oreo cookies out for Scott, who most nights came home late after carousing with friends or spending time with a girlfriend, pay-girl, or stripper. A former boyfriend of Kim's told Ms. North Beach that Kim had an entire Oreo routine when she worked as a bartender at Blue Martini: "Kim put an Oreo cookie between her breasts and then took it out," she said. "You would eat it with a shot of alcohol."

According to Ms. North Beach, however forced the relationship between Scott and Kim may have been, there is

Kim and Scott Rothstein. (Courtesy South Florida Business Journal)

no doubt he admired his wife. "He always used to talk highly about Kim and her family," she said. "And the karate she did. He talked highly about her father. They got along very well. Kim and her father were close."

Scott told Ms. North Beach about how he had set up the warehouse where he stored his cars, out near the airport, with a party room, complete with a pool table, sound system, bar, "and a lot of women. He used to fly people in and fly people out. It was easy access." She also knew about the apartment at 350 East Las Olas Place, where Scott hired escorts for his use and that of some of the lawyers at RRA and to impress and seduce investors. During the December 2011 bankruptcy court deposition, Scott testified that he spent $50,000 to $60,000 per month on prostitutes for himself and others. But Ms. North Beach believes it was less out of cold calculation than an inherent, almost pathological willingness to please. "I think he would do anything that people wanted him to do," she said. "That was his personality. If they asked him, he would try to make it happen. He was the biggest people pleaser I've ever met in the world."

Scott trusted Ms. North Beach so much that he answered her question about the sexuality of his most powerful close friend, Governor Charlie Crist. A trim, dapper man with a dramatic shock of cropped white hair, Crist endured persistent rumors about his sexual orientation throughout his time in high state offices, first as attorney general and later as governor. A moderate Republican, he was particularly vulnerable to rumors of homosexuality. He also suffered whispers that he had fathered a child out of wedlock, and he publically dated beautiful women and married his second wife, businesswoman Carol Rome, in December 2008 while still serving in the governor's mansion. In 2009, however, he was among those "outted" by the controversial film *Outrage,* which attacked

Governor Charlie Crist, Carole Rome, Kim Rothstein, and Scott Rothstein at the 2008 Governor's Ball.

conservative anti-gay politicians it alleged were, in fact, homosexual themselves.

Ms. North Beach asked Scott straight out one day about Charlie Crist. "When you ask someone a question and they hesitate, then there's no certainty," she said. "But when I asked Scott, 'Is Charlie Crist gay?', he had no hesitation. He said, 'Yes, he is.' Scott was so matter of fact about it." For the record, Crist has maintained consistently that he is heterosexual.

Ms. North Beach believes that Scott revealed so much because he trusted her to someday tell his story. "And he knew I'd tell the truth," she said. "He's a smart man and he knew it would all come down."

As 2008 rolled into 2009, the pressure on Scott only grew, and with it grew his spending, his charitable contributions, and his grandiosity. "Things spiraled out of control," Scott wrote in his mitigation letter to Judge Cohn. "But again, I never sincerely tried to stop. I kept telling myself that I would be ok. That everyone was making a lot of money, that our 'investors' were happy, and that ultimately my exit strategy would come to fruition and we would pay everyone off." Scott admits that many of the outside businesses he acquired, "solely to line our pockets and maintain the fraud," were often "just additional sinking ships to fund. And fund them we did . . . with stolen money." In those last few months, Scott told Judge Cohn, he spent "almost every waking hour" trying to keep the Ponzi scheme from blowing up in his face. "It was constantly on the verge of collapse. And yet, I never even tried to stop the bleeding. I kept spending like it was really my money: more expensive cars, boats, offices, jewelry . . . increasing the firm's payroll to ridiculous, unsustainable levels . . . all the trappings of wealth. I gave money to everyone: family, friends, charities. Money that was not mine to give. I convinced myself that my exit strategy would work. It was my only hope. I kept telling myself that I just needed to hang on for a few months."

Eventually, according to Scott's mitigation letter, he came to place all his hopes with the Internet company Qtask. He spent millions of dollars to acquire a significant stake in Qtask, convinced it was poised to "make a killing." Then he could cash out, pay off his investors, and wind down the Ponzi scheme. Alas, things did not work out quite that way. Instead, as his desperation grew, he spent ever more lavishly to "generate a temporary euphoria," Scott wrote. "The Ponzi scheme money [was] like a drug to me. But the high only lasted until the next round of payments was due to my 'investors.'"

Another longtime girlfriend, Ms. Lauderdale, also noticed the price Scott paid to keep his glamorous life intact. A much younger businesswoman, Ms. Lauderdale fell hard for Scott.

"It's fascinating how he lived his life, all the lies," observed Ms. Lauderdale. "I think there is some disease that people have where they can never get enough of a high. Some form of depression. I think he truly had that. I think he could not stop." After Rothstein married Kim, Ms. Lauderdale retained a strong emotional attachment to him, and although the relationship became platonic, the two met for breakfast each Friday at La Bonne Crêpe on Las Olas Boulevard. She observed first hand as Scott's personality was warped by greed, corruption, and pressure. "He was more down to earth, more good-hearted when we were together in 2006 and 2007. Toward the end, it was all about his image. I remember one time I was with him and I asked how he was doing with the piano. Scott said to me, 'I haven't played the piano for a year and a half.' There was a time, before we'd go out and I was getting ready, he'd be downstairs playing the piano. I'd sit on the bench with Scott and he'd play. He loved it. In 2007, he'd play for me all the time."

As summer 2009 edged into fall—a slight lessening of the humidity, a gradual ease toward more Mediterranean temperatures—Scott could see catastrophe looming before him. Not even his mania, greed, and capacity for self-delusion could obscure it. He stopped paying bills, or delayed them as long as possible. Creditors and suppliers, angered at late payments, put Bova Prime on a cash-only basis. Scott could see the day coming soon when he would be unable to meet the scheduled payments of tens of millions of dollars to investors. The end was near.

Chapter 11

Scott's Final Act

Scott admitted that he did everything possible to create a "myth" of power and influence in hopes of holding himself above the law. His admission came in the mitigation letter that he wrote for Judge Cohn. But even here, trying his hardest to appear sincere and contrite and thereby cajole the judge into trimming his sentence, Scott could not prevent his ego from smirking over his shoulder: "I was a criminal. I defrauded people I loved. I gave to charities in enormous amounts thinking I was helping them, when in the end I was just hurting them. *I created a power structure unlike any in Broward County*" (author's emphasis). And he did, but only for a grand total of four years. That is what makes the mitigation letter so fascinating and so useful in the absence of fresh access to the post-downfall Rothstein. No matter how self-serving he might be, glimpses of his real thoughts and feelings keep peeking through. As the Ponzi scheme grew and it became harder and harder to keep it from flying to pieces, Scott became increasingly more stressed: "And ultimately, I did what just several years ago would have been unthinkable to me . . . I forged signatures of sitting judges on orders that I created to convince these kind people who trusted me to part with their money. For what . . . to save myself. I was very near the end."

One of the tools so useful in building that myth, the press, suddenly ceased to cooperate with Rothstein midway through 2009. Rothstein and RRA continued to receive positive coverage for their charitable giving and social prominence—

which, if anything, accelerated as Scott's empire disinte-grated. On October 15, only a fortnight before the scandal dropped, the Signature Chefs & Wine Extravaganza fundraiser for the March of Dimes took place, sponsored by RRA and presented by Rothstein himself. But reporters such as Bob Norman were starting to ask uncomfortable questions. Just a year ago, Norman had written his "This Is Where the Evil Happens" profile, which more than gave Scott the benefit of the doubt. Now, irritated by Norman's persistent digging, Scott made the most condemning of PR mistakes—he called a reporter to berate and threaten him. Norman, of course, took notes. It all appeared in his blog.

Norman's blog post, titled "Scott Rothstein Calls Himself 'Jewish Avenger,' Out to Destroy the Pulp," ran September 2, 2009. It detailed the "seething" phone call in which Rothstein threatened to sue Norman, bankrupt his "household," and bring all his "legal might" to bear on ruining the reporter's career. "Most people figure if you're left alone, you'll go away," Rothstein told Norman. "They figure they should let a sleeping dog lie. I like to jab the dog in the eye. And if it bites me, I'll jab its eye out." A tough journalist who has proven his mettle again and again, Norman was shaken—who wouldn't be, given Rothstein's perceived power at the time—but not cowed. Though the phone call was like "being mugged by a gang of hooligans in Central Park," he stood up to Rothstein, challenging the lawyer on every point. Norman got the last laugh—by simply reporting the exchange, he allowed Rothstein to show more of his frayed state of mind than he surely intended. Scott came off as more than a little unhinged.

The spark that ignited the phone call was almost trivial. Norman had phoned State Representative Evan Jenne, a Democrat from Dania Beach. Jenne worked as a consultant, and Norman had called to dig into his claim that none of the companies with whom he worked had state business.

Norman quizzed Jenne on $30,000 he had earned from Edify, a healthcare firm in which Rothstein happened to be an investor. Norman's interview with Jenne was run-of-mill daily journalism that turned up no evidence of wrongdoing. Its innocence made it interesting enough to report. Only two hours after hanging up with Jenne, Norman received the fire-breathing call from Rothstein. When Scott's initial outburst met resistance, he calmed down and even denied that he had threatened to take Norman's house. "I told you I was going to bankrupt you," he said calmly. "I can't get your house because of homestead laws." It was during this part of the exchange that Scott referred to himself as "the Jewish Avenger," a faux superhero reference that generated gleeful and prolonged mockery in message boards and chat rooms after the Ponzi scheme came to light.

Dr. Joan Pastor, the Beverly Hills clinical and industrial psychologist, commented on this phone exchange, particularly the bizarre "Jewish Avenger" persona, at my request. She suggested the confrontation with Norman provides a window into Scott's mental and emotional make-up. For example, she said people of the Jewish faith—and Dr. Pastor is Jewish herself—often identify strongly with a cohesive Jewish community, even if they are not religious. Scott, as we've seen, was by all accounts quite serious about his faith and its practice. And yet, Rothstein exploited and defrauded other Jews. "It makes me wonder then how much he really does care about his faith," Dr. Pastor said, "Or is it that he uses his ethnicity or faith only when it serves him to do so?" The "Jewish Avenger" title is, she said, frankly odd. "Perhaps the grandiosity that the narcissistic part in him feels led to giving himself a grandiose title which he thought would make him look threatening, superior, and bigger-than-life to Norman." It is common for people with narcissism to feel a "tremendous need to be heard, especially when they have been attacked and feel anxious," she said. And in the summer of 2009, he had plenty of reason to feel both.

"Whatever the reasons behind bringing his Jewish identity into the conversation, the confrontation is also very telling about Rothstein's personality structure," Pastor said. "If he was only a brilliant psychopath, he would either have ignored Norman or would have been able to keep his emotions in tight control in the confrontation. That would have accomplished more and he wouldn't have looked so foolish." In the long run, she concluded, both Scott's narcissistic and psychopathic facets were in play during the confrontation with Norman. The threats levied against the reporter are indications of antisocial personality disorder, while the grandiosity and emotionality are expressions of narcissism. Even so, an intelligent, inventive person with a personality disorder can instinctively know how to use his "shallow emotionality" to "create a certain impression," as Scott did during his phone call.

A chance remark by Norman set Rothstein off another tirade that ended in Rothstein calling the reporter a "m----- f-----" and hanging up. Thirty seconds later, Scott called again, this time with an entirely different persona, and asked, "Bob, you want to try to be polite now?" He proceeded to detail, in reasonable tones, his plans to reign in journalists such as Norman, some at the *Sun Sentinel,* including Norman's wife, investigative reporter Brittany Wallman: "The unfortunate thing is that the news media, including you, has taken a terrible turn, and I find it appalling. I am going to open up my wallet to offer legal representation to anyone who you have harmed." Uncowed, Norman was left wondering how many of Scott's vaunted forty-three personalities he had just been talking with—it seems to have been at least three. His conclusion was hard-nosed and practical, however: "It seems to me that Rothstein simply wants to control the way he is covered by the media, and throwing fits and threatening lawsuits is part of his strategy. The first time I ever spoke to him, he said that if I ever wrote anything unfactual about him, he would 'live in [my] house.' Yes, it was a threat."

While Rothstein's response to invasive media coverage is valid, his call to Norman was simply an attempt to intimidate a pesky reporter into backing off. In retrospect, however, another aspect of the conversation became quite obvious: why he said what he said. Striving with all his might to hold his legal and business empire together, Scott was terrified that the smallest amount of unfriendly press might undermine his chances of attracting fresh investors into the Ponzi scheme. He was terrified that the Ponzi scheme was about to tumble into ruin.

Scott had plenty of reason to be worried. While he lived large in public, spending money, investing in companies, supporting a wide range of society charities, and donating money to political candidates, his empire was crumbling from the inside as early as January 2009. That month, he bought a lot across the street from his Harbor Beach mansion for $4 million, but it was the last of the grand real estate gestures, the kind that had characterized the previous year. In 2008, Rothstein purchased seven big-ticket properties, from South Florida to Manhattan to Newport Beach, Rhode Island, at a total cost of $17 million, overpaying for each one in a sharply declining real estate market. A *Sun Sentinel* story by Sally Kestin and Peter Franceschina reported that Scott's Ponzi scheme had gained momentum slowly from its inception in 2005, but by the middle of 2008, it had started to take off. As a result, Rothstein found himself awash in money, on the one hand, in constant need of large infusions of cash in a very short period of time to keep up payments to his investors. The Ed Morse scam came in March of that year, when Rothstein forged court documents and lied to his client in order to steal $57 million from the car dealership kingpin. Scott seems to have plowed most of that considerable fortune into the Ponzi scheme, according to then-acting US Attorney Jeffrey Sloman. A former US Treasury agent, Bill Branscum, characterized the Morse scam to the *Sun Sentinel* as an act of desperation. "They always reach a point where they realize they can't sustain what they are doing, that it is all flowing the wrong way," Branscum said. "Then the panic sets in."

At the same time, Scott set up dozens of companies, many of them incorporated in Delaware, into which he could transfer ownership of his real estate and other assets. In January 2006, on one day alone he formed sixteen corporations. This flurry of activity suggests that Scott was thinking about an exit strategy that would allow him to escape the inevitable crash with his wealth and freedom intact. Apparently, he intended to hide assets. After his downfall, federal investigators called Scott's transfer of assets into dummy corporations "a wealth preservation mechanism." As Boston University Journalism Professor Mitchell Zuckoff told the *Sun Sentinel,* Rothstein's frantic actions were common to Ponzi schemers. "The door was closing," Zuckoff said. "These guys do often at the end become deeply desperate."

Needing to attract new investors into the Ponzi scheme, Scott forged and altered documents from TD Bank, where he had been a VIP customer since 2007 due to the large account balances he kept there. According to bankruptcy court testimonies given by TD Bank officials in May 2010, account balance information was emailed to William "Bill Brock" Boockvor, Scott's Uncle Bill. Roseanne Caretsky, Weston branch manager, testified that when she saw a copy of the electronic balances after Scott's fall, the numbers had been changed to show hundreds of millions of dollars that were not, in fact, in the accounts. "I saw documents that were altered, and it had to be from that original e-mail," she testified. One electronic balance, for example, listed $58 million but was missing the date and time stamp necessary to establish its authenticity. Rothstein used these bogus accounts, but he also paid his IT technician to create an entire false TD Bank website, and his friend Stephen Caputi sometimes posed as a bank official in meetings with prospective investors. In November 2011, two full years after the Ponzi scheme collapsed, Boockvor became the eighth person indicted in the fallout of Scott's Ponzi scheme. He pleaded guilty on February 8, 2012, just more than two years after Rothstein's brief flight to Morocco. Uncle Bill's charges included wire fraud.

Scott bullied and manipulated his two principle banks, TD Bank, where he did most of his business, and Gibraltar Private Bank & Trust, from the inception of the Ponzi scheme in 2005. By threatening to go elsewhere with his business and take his rich client list with him, he was able to write bad checks and have them honored. Eventually, everything that he owed would catch up with him. As the *South Florida Business Journal* reported, Gibraltar earned $200,000 in fees on approximately $64 million of overdrafts that the bank honored for Rothstein, albeit reluctantly. In response to suits filed by Ponzi scheme victims, Gibraltar released emails from Rothstein in which he threatened to take business elsewhere, even though he had purchased a five-percent stake in the bank, a tactic that also earned Scott special privileges.

The crafty Rothstein wielded the carrot as well as the stick, however, wining and dining bank officials. The mixture worked. One investors' suit alleged that Gibraltar Chairman and CEO, Steven Hayworth, directly protected RRA from a bank compliance officer's inquiry about transactions in the firm's account. In 2010, federal regulators cited the bank for weak anti-money laundering compliance, citing "unsafe and unsound" practices and "ineffective" compliance with the Bank Secrecy Act. In November 2011, bankruptcy trustee Howard Stettin, seeking to recover payments for victims of the Ponzi scheme, filed a rash of new lawsuits, including one alleging that former Gibraltar officers John Harris, Charles "Chuck" Sanders, and Lisa Ellis were aware that Rothstein's accounts violated banking regulations. Stettin's suit claimed these bank officers went further, actively impeding inquiries by another bank official, Julie Ansari. Employing his carrot-and-stick strategy, Scott was able to treat both institutions as if they were his private piggy-banks. Shielded from most customary oversight, he not only falsified account balances to deceive new investors and wrote bad checks with huge numbers on them, but also he freely moved funds out of trust accounts set up to protect investors' money and into private ones for his own use. Needless to say, this is all illegal.

Nonetheless, Rothstein found it necessary to engage in a constant battle with Gibraltar and TD Bank concerning overdrafts. Some officials at each bank tried to do their jobs, much to Scott's irritation. In the early years, his emails were cocky, such as this one from 2006 regarding overdrafts:

> If they are going to start putting pressure on us again every time the account is od [overdrawn] from the previous nights pod they can kiss my firm, my consulting group, Albert, Ovi, Ovi's dad, Roger, the Bahamas deal and all the rest that goes with me goodbye . . . I will not be pushed or pressured by the idiots in credit ever again. Not for one second. And you can tell them if they screw around with me I will be sure to tell every other one of their clients that I represent and that I am close to exactly what they are doing.

This kind of bullying went on regularly, right through the pressures of 2009. By then, however, weariness can be detected in Scott's emails: "I do not believe that I am being treated as valued customer by Gibraltar and candidly, it has grown tiresome. . . . I also intend to meet with Stu and David Boden in the morning to discuss ending my banking relationship with Gibraltar."

The toll taken on Rothstein by the stress of trying to hold the Ponzi scheme together was obvious to those closest to him. They might not have known he was frantically searching for new investors, alternately hoping for a score that would make everything right—his unrealistic bet on Qtask, for example— while trying to orchestrate an exit strategy. But they noticed the tension. His tic, always a part of the Rothstein persona, grew much more pronounced. Ms. North Beach, one of his closest girlfriends, noticed the change. "He had more ADD," she recalled. "His attention span faded, it was terrible. He was pulled in so many different directions. It was not the normal Scott I knew. His twitching got worse. He would sit and talk to me and his whole head would twitch." One night, four months before the implosion, Scott took Ms. North Beach to the Las Olas apartment. "Scott wanted to tell me something that day, and he took me there because I was moving out of my house," she said. "We walked together over there. Nothing happened between us. He was sitting there on the couch, but he never could quite get it out, what he wanted to say."

Unaware of the Ponzi scheme, she attributed Scott's stress to unseen organized crime business partners. "My suspicions were the Mafia," she said. "As for all that other stuff, no. Definitely the Mafia, after he told me about his past and his father. He said his real father was Bugsy Siegel, and he romanticized where he grew up in New York, with the gangsters around the neighborhood. A lot of friends talked to me about Scott's involvement with the Mafia, but I said to them, 'I love Scott.'" The Bugsy-Siegel-was-my-dad story is typical of the glamorous but tissue-thin self-mythologizing Scott liked to indulge in. Benjamin Siegelbaum was the Brooklyn-born Jewish gangster associated with the Genovese crime family who developed Las Vegas into the casino mecca we know today. He was assassinated in an apparent mob hit in Beverly Hills, California, in 1947, fifteen years before Scott Rothstein was born.

Ms. Lauderdale, the younger woman who was at one time the love of Scott's life, noticed the change, too. She broke up with him when he married Kim, but he pursued a platonic relationship, and after a couple of months, she gave in. She agreed to meet him once per week for breakfast. Scott told her that he had to pick Kim for practical reasons, but he needed her in his life. "He said, 'Look, she's not going to ask questions and I still need to see you on a weekly basis because I've never felt so loved by somebody like I do by you.'" Even after they stopped being a couple, Ms. Lauderdale thought she knew Scott. "But as the years went on, and we went our separate ways, he completely changed, one hundred percent. He used to be more down-to-earth, more good-hearted. Toward the end, it was more about his image and keeping up with the Joneses." She was especially saddened when she learned he had all but given up his interest in music, abandoning the piano that had been among the things that charmed her in the first place.

It is no wonder that Rothstein gave up his musical pursuits with a schedule full of charity and political fundraisers, multiple girlfriends, and confronting one business or legal crisis after another. For example, in February 2009, a pair of investors, Gerald Brauser and Leon Brauser, threatened to go public when they discovered that the money that they had invested with Rothstein was not being held in escrow, as it was supposed to be. According to a $37.7 million suit filed by bankruptcy trustee Herbert Stettin in October 2011 against Rothstein's general counsel, David Boden, Scott paid the Brausers $4.2 million out of an RRA account. A settlement agreement prepared by Boden, stipulated that the Brausers verify they had not, in fact, gone to the authorities. The

Scott Rothstein next to his piano in his Harbor Beach home.

agreement "created safeguards to limit" the investors from "cooperating with anyone about the affairs of RRA, so as to assure absolute secrecy on the Brauser settlement and the Ponzi scheme, which enabled it to continue for eight more months." As the *Sun Sentinel* reported, the suit accuses Boden, who famously wept in an earlier deposition as he attempted to paint himself as another of Scott's victims, of being fully aware of and therefore complicit in the Ponzi scheme.

One of Boden's duties at RRA was to verify investments for the benefit of investors. Stettin's clawback suit alleged: "Of course Boden never took steps to verify anything, because the money was not in the bank accounts, which he would have discovered, had he looked.... In fact, a cursory examination of RRA's corporate financial books and the RRA bank account would have revealed that the sale of pre-trial settlements was fraudulent, because the money that was supposed to be in those accounts was not there and the supposed clients did not exist. This is further evidence of Boden's actual knowledge of Rothstein's fraud and Boden's direct complicity in the Ponzi scheme." In essence, though it may not have seemed so nefarious to the Brausers at the time, Scott in effect bought their silence with the $4 million payout. Otherwise, the Ponzi scheme would have collapsed and Scott would have been exposed as a crook nine months earlier.

Another co-conspirator, who is alleged to have worked diligently to keep the Ponzi scheme secret and thriving, according to the closed-door testimony that Rothstein gave in December 2011, was his old friend Ted Morse. The government, which holds Rothstein in prison under the Witness Protection Program, brought Scott to an eleventh-floor courtroom in the James Lawrence King Federal Justice Building in downtown Miami, where approximately thirty-five lawyers, representing investors scorched by the Ponzi scheme, as well as Charles Lichtman, one of the lawyers for the bankruptcy trustees, lined up to ask him questions. Also present were Assistant US District Attorney Lawrence LaVecchio, who made sure Scott said nothing about his alleged association with mobsters or his corruption of cops, politicians, and judges, and Rothstein's attorney, Marc Nurik, a partner at RRA before the crash. The attorneys had been anxious to get access to Rothstein since his sentence of fifty years of imprisonment in July 2010. Ever the self-interested showman, Rothstein did his best to oblige. According to lawyers in the room (the press was barred, although transcripts were made public by the presiding jurist, US Bankruptcy Court Judge Raymond Ray), Rothstein hoped that cooperating with authorities will shave time off of his prison sentence. Reportedly, almost the first thing he said was, "I don't want to die in prison." This came in response to the question of why anyone should believe him. "I would be a fool," Rothstein said. "I would be a fool to lie." Then Scott proceeded to apportion blame to Stuart Rosenfeldt and Russell Adler, the two other name partners at RRA, plus a trio of independent lawyers, TD bank executive Frank Spinosa, and most notably his closest friend, Ted Morse.

The investors' attorney, William Scherer, filed suit almost immediately, alleging that Morse, scion of the Morse car dealership empire founded by his father, Ed, in 1946, was "a charter member of Rothstein's Ponzi scheme." Scherer's suit claimed that Morse was a "co-conspirator" who "knew Rothstein was running a fraudulent scheme and provided substantial assistance to it." Using accounts he allegedly kept secret from his wife and parents, Ted Morse secretly shuttled nearly $37 million of family money out of Morse Operations Inc. and into the Ponzi scheme between 2006 and 2009, enabling Scott to pay off previous investors during lean times, thereby keeping the fraud afloat. Morse received his investment back, plus some $13 million in profit, according to court filings. Rothstein paid an interest rate as high as 235 percent. Most damaging to Morse is Scherer's allegation that he actively abetted Rothstein in early 2009 into stealing $57 million from Morse's parents in the infamous interior decorator suit.

While Rothstein's testimony and the allegations detailed in the new bankruptcy suits against Ted Morse may seem persuasive, I strongly believe that Scott cannot be trusted to testify truthfully, no matter how much he wants to get out of jail before he dies—in fact, trumping up other charges could prove in his favor. After having read the transcripts, his pathological ego seemed to be in full flower at times during his testimony in December 2011. Simply put, the more convictions his cooperation can bring to the Justice Department, the harder government lawyers will lobby Judge Cohn to reduce his sentence.

I do not know Ted Morse well and have no direct opinion on his guilt or innocence or the degree of his involvement in the Ponzi scheme. But I do know Stuart Rosenfeldt, and I cannot credit Rothstein's assertion that he was a passive partner in the financial crimes perpetrated at RRA. Of Rosenfeldt and Adler, Rothstein said, "They knew that we were moving money illegally in and out of the law firm. At various points in time, they came to know that there was a Ponzi scheme going on, although the word Ponzi was never utilized."

Of Rosenfeldt individually, Rothstein testified, "Stu was in a unique position. Stu was not directly involved in the Ponzi scheme, other than to live the lifestyle. At some point in time he became aware that we were selling the illegal settlements. He tried at one point in time, to my knowledge, to attempt to bring an investor in. Other than that, you know, he wasn't involved on a daily basis except to reap the rewards from it."

Scott's testimony included he spent $60,000 a month on escorts for himself, his friends, his lawyers, investors, and police. Rothstein was quick to throw a couple of his partners under the bus with allegations that RRA attorneys participated with escorts.

"We had a condo in 350 Las Olas right across the street from the office," Rothstein testified. "That's where . . . we would send a girl up there, and then we'd go up there and do our business and come back to work."

Not surprisingly, attorneys representing all of Rothstein's former partners and associates named as participants in these sexcapades responded vigorously. Fred Haddad, Adler's attorney, said, according to the *Sun Sentinel*, "What else would you expect from Rothstein? He's keeping the fraud going. He's defrauding the government with his testimony and they are buying it." Boden's attorney, David Vinikoor, kept it simple: "It's ludicrous." Christopher Berga, representing Szafranski, issued a written statement, saying, in part, "It is bad enough that Mr. Szafranski has had to endure all of Rothstein's other false allegations that he was a co-conspirator in the fraud, but an assault on a man's marriage, particularly when false, goes too far."

I do not know if Rothstein's allegations of hookers being used by Szafranski, Boden, Adler, or Ted Morse are true. Certainly, some—perhaps most—of his statements are true, but everything he says, even under oath, needs to be sifted finely before we accept its veracity.

Despite Morse's alleged support—his attorneys assert that Rothstein is lying—the Ponzi scheme sputtered, wheezed, and flew out of control like a car engine blowing a rod. The $57 million bilked from Ed Morse, with or without son Ted's connivance, could only stave off the inevitable for a surprisingly brief period as Scott struggled to find the big payout that would enable him to wind down the Ponzi scheme.

That eventuality, never very likely, became ever more remote, and as it did, Scott's mental state deteriorated.

Though Stuart Rosenfeldt remained confident of his more dynamic partner until the end, he did grow disgusted with Scott's antics. "In later years I thought it was silly, with the bodyguards and everything. He became a caricature of himself. I asked, 'Do I need a bodyguard and is there something you haven't told me?' He said, 'No, I live ostentatiously. John McCain advised that I should have a bodyguard.'" Rosenfeldt also was annoyed when Scott turned his inner suite of offices at RRA into what became known as "the bunker," with its own keycard system and security cameras. It was in October 2008, just as things were cresting for Scott and the downhill slide was about to commence, that Rosenfeldt informed Rothstein that he planned to leave the firm. Among other things, Stuart was annoyed by the way Scott cut him out of all real decision-making responsibilities, even though they were supposed to be partners. He was supposed to have card access to the bunker, for example, but sometimes it would be turned off, which irked Stuart to no end. Scott wept, begging him to stay, and Stuart relented.

In Scott's mitigation letter to Judge Cohn, he suggested that money had become a kind of drug to him, the getting and spending of it a kind of addiction. "I never sincerely attempted to stop," he said. Scott eventually placed all his hopes of escape on the Internet company Qtask and its proprietary legal project software, certain it "was going to make a killing. At least I convinced myself of that. Just another lie that I told myself to justify my spending and my greed." Instead, Rothstein said, he eventually "would bottom out mentally and spend like there was no tomorrow to generate a temporary euphoria. . . . But the high only lasted until the next round of payments was due."

The increasing fragmentation of Scott's mind can be traced in the "love ya" emails he sent to his colleagues and employees at RRA. Another thing Rosenfeldt didn't know, at least not until after the Ponzi scheme failed and Scott fled to Morocco, was that Rothstein had forged Rosenfeldt's signature on a personal guarantee for new office space. "It was the first I'd heard of it," says Rosenfeldt. "One of the ironies here is that if Scott had asked me to sign the personal guarantee, I would have."

Those lawyers who knew what Stuart, the partner, did not, jostled for the best office spaces on the new floor. Some of them tried to go around Debra Villegas, the firm's COO, to lobby Scott directly. Scott was not pleased. He sent out a companywide email dated March 23, 2009, to affirm Debra's authority as the firm's Number Two. He started reasonably: "In order to insure that RRA runs as smoothly as possible, and in light of multiple recent incidents pertaining to Debra's role at RRA, let's define certain responsibilities of her position clearly . . . [W]hen she speaks she is speaking for me . . . [N]o one is to challenge her authority or come to me to attempt to override any decision she makes." Near the end, however, Scott slipped into an all-caps outburst: "WE WOULD NOT EXIST WITHOUT HER . . . SHE HAS HELPED ME AND CONTINUES TO HELP ME MORE THAN I COULD EVER EXPLAIN . . ." He continued like that for a long paragraph, before closing with his customary "Love ya, Me." Apparently the message didn't get through. Six months later, on October 16, 2009—less than two weeks before the end—Scott sent out a less tempered email, almost all of it in capitals:

I AM THE CHAIRMAN . . . THE CEO . . . THE MANAGING SHAREHOLDER . . . AND THE HEAD JANITOR. DEBRA IS THE COO . . . SHE IS SECOND IN COMMAND. MAKE NO MISTAKE ABOUT IT. SHE IS . . . AND SHE ONLY ANSWERS TO ME. NO ONE ELSE. END OF STORY. DO NOT CROSS THE LINE. IF YOU ARE NOT IN MANAGEMENT MAKE NO ATTEMPT TO MANAGE . . . PLEASE. I AM SO ANGRY THAT I AM HAVING TO WRITE THIS EMAIL. WE HAVE AN AMAZING FIRM . . .

AN AMAZING WORKPLACE . . . STOP PISSING ME OFF.
IT WILL NOT GET YOU ANYWHERE THAT YOU WANT
TO BE. PLEASE.

Scott even used all capitals when he signed off: "LOVE YA, Scott." As capital letters is the email equivalent of shouting, this message bordered on hysteria. Who would not be hysterical when a gigantic and illegal empire is about to collapse?

Even as Scott spent ever-vaster sums, his Ponzi scheme sputtered like an engine running out of gas. According to a lawsuit filed by investors' attorney William Scherer, managers at two New York hedge funds, Centurion and Platinum, realized early in 2009 that Rothstein's investment scheme was fraudulent. Rather than exposing Rothstein, the funds concocted a strategy to keep silent and "secure the withdrawal [of their money] from the Ponzi." The funds discovered Scott's problems when he was able to make only partial payments to Platinum and Centurion in April. The two hedge funds had invested through George Levin's Banyon Income Fund, a so-called feeder fund that did so much business with Rothstein that Frank Preve, Banyon's COO, had an office at RRA. Acting as a go-between, Preve applied pressure on Rothstein as best he could. After Preve received an email from Platinum, questioning in detail the missing payment of more than $7 million—Rothstein had sent a partial payment of $256,000— he, in turn, emailed Rothstein. "This is exactly what we needed to avoid," wrote an alarmed Preve. "Between the call to Mayer [Nordlicht, at Centurion] and this wire, we have opened the floodgates of doubt. Why send them anything if we are going to only send them $256k??" Rothstein borrowed $15 million to pay Platinum, but that only spurred the two funds to get whatever additional payouts they could while keeping the situation secret from their own investors.

Scott, still cocky, played tough with the hedge funds. In a May 6 email to Nordlicht, he warned the hedge funds against issuing a default against Banyon, which would effectively have been the same as issuing against Rothstein: "I am certain that given all of our conversations and all that has transpired, you understand that such an act would serve no one's purpose, with a result none of us want." Throughout May, Rothstein fell farther and farther behind in its payments to Centurion and Platinum—$1.5 million here, $1.5 million there. When Preve forwarded a fairly gentle email from Centurion, Scott reacted brusquely: "What the hell is that b------- about u being concerned about the lack of direct releases . . . u make me sound like the problem. And I didn't start this s---. Don't hang me out to dry with these m------------."

By borrowing money to make some payments and a mixture of bluffing and cajolery, Rothstein was able to keep the teetering Ponzi empire upright for four more months. As summer 2009 edged into fall, Scott began moving vast sums around—as much as $200 million in October alone, according to Scherer, who said that between May and October some $100 million belonging to investor Doug Van Allmen vanished down the rabbit hole of Rothstein's accounts. By the middle of October, a now-frantic Scott could no longer deny the likelihood the Ponzi scheme was in danger of imminent collapse. On Saturday, October 17, 2009, he sent emergency emails to RRA lawyers, asking for someone to research a bizarre point of law: what countries do not have extradition treaties with either the United States or Israel. "We have a client that was a United States citizen until about 6 months ago. He became a citizen of Israel and renounced his United States citizenship. He is likely to be charged with a multitude of crimes in the United States including fraud, money laundering, and embezzlement." He added: "This client is related to a very powerful client of ours and so time is of the essence. Lets rock and roll . . . there is a very large fee attached to this case. Thanks. Love ya, Scott." His lawyers replied promptly, saying that the recent Israeli citizenship would likely be rescinded, if it was deemed obtained "to evade prosecution." Scott was also warned that the "client" must be willing to stay in the new country "for the rest of his life," because electronic passports then being implemented worldwide track by fingerprints, not nationality. "He wants to avoid being a 'Roman Polanski' in thirty years," one RRA attorney wrote. In the end, one lawyer related that Morocco is the only country without an extradition treaty to the United States or Israel.

Scott began making plans to escape to Morocco at once. But first, as he told Judge Cohn in the mitigation letter, he considered a faster way out of his troubles. Just days before flying to Morocco at the end of October, Rothstein sat in the shower at his Harbor Beach mansion, dressed in a suit, pressing the barrel of a .357 magnum to his head as he wept and tried to work up the nerve. "I sat there for well over an hour. Telling myself repeatedly to just pull the trigger and end the pain. Everyone would be better off. And of course, being the considerate husband, I went into the shower so that my wife would not have to deal with the mess my final selfish act would leave behind." Instead, however, he decided to go forward with the Morocco plan. Scott informed Kim he had business outside the country, chartered a jet, and arranged to have Uncle Bill travel with him. He packed and waited for his wife to come home. When she arrived, he kissed her goodbye and left.

This self-serving account has an air of accuracy, but Kim is not the only woman he kissed on the way out of town. Ms. North Beach told a story that suggests that Scott's flight to Morocco might not have been quite as impulsive as he wanted Judge Cohn to believe. One day toward the end of October, she recalled, she sat at the bar at Bova in the company of a couple of attorneys. "Typically at Bova, Scott is pretty normal," she said. "He waves 'Hi,' but because of Kim he wouldn't pay much attention to me. He would say hi from a distance." On this occasion, however, Scott entered the restaurant and walked directly to her. Others noticed, too, she said. Scott said, "Everything is going to be okay," and then he gave her a passionate kiss. Then he walked away. "I turned to my friend and I specifically said, 'Was that the kiss of death?'" Even today, after the fact, Ms. North Beach believes that Scott was sending her a message. "It wasn't the kiss of death, it was a kiss good-bye. I wonder how many other women he kissed good-bye like that? I know mine was important. I'm sure there were a few others."

On the very night Scott was scheduled to host the first major South Florida charity event of the fall season of 2009, he was instead winging his way east across the South Atlantic. By his side sat the loyal Uncle Bill. In his luggage were nestled cash and several million dollars worth of luxury watches. In an overseas bank account, he had spirited away somewhere between $15 million and $18 million—accounts vary—not enough to match his lifestyle of the past four years, but a sufficient number, or so he hoped, to establish a safe and comfortable life for himself in the only place where he could be sure American justice could not reach him.

Chapter 12

Morocco, the Mob, the Rat

Two days before Scott Rothstein climbed into a private jet on October 27, 2009, and took flight to Morocco, he failed to make big scheduled payments to investors. This was, in fact, only the most recent of a mounting series of missed or partial payments that had started early in the year and continued throughout 2009, as evidenced by increasingly panicked emails sent to Rothstein from Frank Preve, the chief operating officer of the Banyon Income Fund, a hedge fund operated by investor George Levin that had funneled more than $700 million into the Ponzi scheme. At one point, a desperate, exasperated Preve wrote in an email, "What is the plan for the next 20 minutes?"

On April 27, 2009 Preve chided Rothstein for floating an "undocumented" rationale to investors for holding up a $30 million payment and apparently offered to make up the shortfall through a bogus "settlement" agreement with Banyon that would make it appear that Rothstein had "defended" his clients. That same day, in a separate email, Preve identified RRA's number one problem as its need of "cover for its non-funding of clients," and suggested an arcane strategy by which Banyon would consent to provide $150 million in the following twenty days with a "personal written guarantee" from George Levin. Obviously, Preve, Levin, and Banyon were desperate to keep Scott's investment schemes afloat, whether they knew that he was running a Ponzi scheme, as the investors' lawyers claim, or not. By May

18, Preve wrote: "I am petrified. [I]f word gets out that we are $125 million past due we will never see another cent in 3rd party funding . . . The fact that I am concerned that 25% of our portfolio is past due should not come as a surprise to you, to the Bar, to God, or to anyone else that notices that I am walking around smelling like [I] just peed my pants." Nonetheless, Preve assured Rothstein, "no one is throwing you under the bus."

Matters only worsened over the summer. By September 15, Preve wrote, "The system is not working . . . yesterday I failed to make $500,000 in payments to our largest investor and it will not be pretty today. In addition, on the 28th we have two loans maturing that cannot be extended—$1.5m and $5.5m—if we don't plan for these in advance." On September 22, Preve, worried by scrutiny "of the cavernous hole that I have allowed to be created," pleaded with Rothstein for documentation of monies paid. In an October 3 email he warned "the crapola [sic] is going to hit the fan" if Scott and Michael Szafranski, the RRA in-house "independent verifier" could not provide sufficient information to calm down Doug Von Allmen. On October 21, barely a week before Scott fled to Morocco, Preve wrote that his ability "to stay afloat with smoke and mirrors is gone." He reminded Rothstein that Banyon had "reinvested and raised about $170,000,000 since the meltdown last April."

The day before he left the country, Scott ate lunch at Bova Prime with Frank Spinosa, the TD Bank vice-president who aided the Ponzi scheme, either unwittingly or, as Scott later testified, as a knowing accomplice. An agitated Richard Pearson, vice-president of the Banyon Fund, interrupted their meal, demanding to know why payments had been missed. Somehow, Rothstein mollified Pearson, who had made millions steering investors into the Ponzi scheme. But Spinosa was left shaken.

Though so gripped by stress that he later testified that he had only a vague memory of the day, Scott comported himself with his customary cool-headedness. He wired $15 million to Morocco in the name of Ahnich Khalid, manager of a Boca Raton Italian restaurant, and completed arrangements to flee the country the following day. A Moroccan native who had lived in the United States for more than twenty-five years, Khalid agreed to accompany Rothstein on the trip as a guide on what he thought was a business scouting trip. Khalid knew Rothstein only as a rich man with an interest in investing in Morocco. He had no inkling of the Ponzi scheme or of Scott's plan to escape American justice. For his part, Rothstein knew the Ponzi scheme was wrecked beyond repair. All his sources of big money—the Morse family, Doug Von Allmen—had already been milked for hundreds of millions of dollars, and new investors could not be brought on board fast enough. What he feared most, what had kept him from a full night's sleep for more than a year, had come to pass. As Scott saw it, he had two alternatives: kill himself or run.

It is a matter of local infamy that a high-ranking official from the Broward Sheriff's Office escorted Rothstein to the Fort Lauderdale Executive Airport, where a chartered private jet awaited. Lieutenant David Benjamin, executive officer to Sheriff Al Lamberti, responded with alacrity when Scott called, even though it was his day off. Why Benjamin agreed to meet Rothstein at the airport and walk him to the tarmac is unclear. Supposedly, Scott told the lieutenant that his regular bodyguard was unavailable. However, for the better part of a year, the extra-duty security details that Scott had hired came from the Fort Lauderdale Police Department, not the Sheriff's Office. It remains to be discovered why Rothstein needed a police escort in the first place. True, he was spiriting $2 million worth of designer watches out of the country and a duffle bag with as much as $3 million in cash, but, according to press accounts, he did not have to clear customs because he was traveling on a private charter. And, he requested Benjamin's company for what must have been the safest part of his trip: through the airport to the plane. Scott would have been most vulnerable to random robbery during the twelve-mile drive from his home on Fort Lauderdale Beach to the Executive Airport on Commercial Boulevard. It seems a reasonable assumption that Scott had some other motive in calling for Benjamin to meet him, even if it was only to tell an old friend—or useful minion—goodbye. A week later, after the Ponzi scandal was public, the Sheriff's spokesman Jim Leljedal told reporter Bob Norman that was the case: "He met him. They walked to the plane, the driver loaded some luggage, and Dave said goodbye. He was doing it as a friend. They have been friends for many years." No word has emerged to date on what might have been said between the two men during this display of masculine bonding and loyalty.

In the messy aftermath of Scott's downfall, Lamberti kicked Benjamin off of his command staff, ostensibly for failing to report the $30,000 Rothstein paid Benjamin's side corporation, DWB Consulting Group. Over the years, Scott had bestowed gifts on Benjamin, too, and as he was about to climb onto the plane he gave the sheriff's lieutenant a costly watch. An internal investigation into Benjamin's activities has continued on since the Ponzi scheme was discovered, with no end in sight. Bob Norman suggested that Lamberti is using the investigation to prevent deputies from talking to the press about the matter on pain of prosecution and dismissal. Lamberti is no stranger to Scott Rothstein, either, having received some $200,000 in campaign donations from Rothstein or his surrogates at RRA. Benjamin continues to work for the Sheriff's Office as director of the Juvenile Assessment Center at his old salary of $106,000 per year. In October 2011, Benjamin settled with the bankruptcy court, agreeing to pay back the $30,000 and return a Choppard watch that Rothstein gave him. The federal government is known to be investigating allegations by Rothstein that he corrupted police and judges in South Florida, but no details as to which officials are under scrutiny have been forthcoming as yet.

Scott took two companions along on the flight to Morocco. Khalid, completely unaware he accompanied the head of a massive criminal enterprise, was to serve as a local guide and business facilitator. Also on board was William Boockvor, Scott's mysterious "Uncle Bill," an employee at RRA and one of Rothstein's closest collaborators on the internal mechanics of the Ponzi scheme. During the investigations since Scott's collapse, Boockvor admitted to having assisted the firm in other accounting capacities, having told one questioner, "I write the checks." Speculation later centered on Boockvor's role in the flight to Morocco and whether he facilitated the offshore transfer of $15 million, whether the cash-filled duffle bag existed, or whether he was purely traveling for "moral" support.

In his mitigation letter to Judge Cohn and in his December 2011 testimony before the bankruptcy court deposition in Miami, Scott portrayed his six days in Morocco as a time of soul searching and anguish. He testified that he was "in a sheer state of panic," worried for the safety of his family, guilt-ridden over the enormous damage he had caused, and contemplating suicide. A text message he sent to George Levin and Frank Preve read in part, "I am in much greater danger than simply dealing with these issues. My life and the lives of my parents, sister, kids and wife are all in jeopardy. Please watch out for yourselves. Despite my idiocy, I love you both. Scott." He sent a message to his partners at RRA that appears to be a suicide note: "Sorry for letting you all down. I am a fool. I thought I could fix it, but got trapped by my ego and refusal to fail, and now all I have accomplished is hurting the people I love. Please take care of yourselves and please protect Kimmie. She knew nothing. Neither did she, nor any of you deserve what I did. I hope God allows me to see you on the other side. Love, Scott."

At one point, Rothstein claims he made another suicide attempt, lining up a series of pills—Xanax and blood pressure medication—which he started washing down with swigs of vodka, his preferred beverage. But he did not go through with it for a complex set of reasons. Stuart Rosenfeldt said Scott called him from Morocco to talk things over with his old partner and friend. "He said he had three choices: life on the run, knowing they'd be out to get him; [to] come back and go to jail for a very long time; or [to] take a bottle of pills and a bottle of vodka that he had with him. All I said was, 'Choose life.'" Scott sent an email to Levin and Preve taking full responsibility for the Ponzi scheme (he later testified that Preve knew exactly what was going on, however): "Do not try to bail me out of this, save yourself . . . I either go to jail or die. Why should I put my family through watching me go to jail? Love forever, Scott." Ironically, Preve had direct acquaintance with Rothstein's situation. According to *Businessweek,* Preve pleaded guilty in 1985 to bank embezzlement and received a sentence of ten years. Preve drew on that experience to encourage Rothstein, writing in an email: "I ran once, but people smarter than me talked sense into me by pointing that my absence would destroy the ones that I loved and was trying to protect. By returning I had to face the shame of my actions, the vengeance of my enemies and the nastiness of our criminal justice system; but I also incurred renewed spirit by the love of my family and support of my friends."

Scott was not the only one in a state of panic—if indeed he was. Back in South Florida, Levin, Preve, and other investors scrambled for ways to keep the Rothstein investment scheme afloat in hopes of getting their money back out of it. To do this, they would have had to raise enough funding to pay off the investors whose loans were currently due. Apparently, Levin was willing to put up hundreds of millions more dollars to keep the investments from failing. On October 31, Preve emailed Scott to say he'd heard $300 million was needed, "which is still manageable if we have your cooperation." Rothstein testified that Levin might have believed a substantial sum remained in the bogus trust accounts, which were in fact empty. Scott, as he told the attorneys gathered for his bankruptcy deposition, knew there was no hope before he left town. "I had actually thrown in the towel. I was scrambling to try to figure out what the heck to do. The only way I really, and it was kind of crazy, the only way I really thought I could be rescued was if George Levin somehow was convinced to do a raise that would have returned the principles at least to these people. But I knew no matter what that if I returned to the United States I was going to prison."

Rothstein's portrayal of himself as angst-ridden and remorsefully suicidal in Morocco contrasts sharply with the happy, relaxed, and rich American businessman Ahnich Khalid accompanied around Morocco. An RRA attorney who knew he was a member of the Moroccan American Coalition, a group that seeks to build relationships between US business interests and Morocco, introduced Khalid to Rothstein. Apparently, she too thought this was to be a legitimate investment scouting trip. Khalid agreed to take a week's vacation to be Scott's guide. As Khalid told *New Times*' Bob Norman, "To me, I was taking an investor to Morocco, not a thief." Khalid agreed to allow Rothstein to wire $40,000 to $50,000 into his Moroccan bank account, but when he arrived in Casablanca, he was shocked to discover $15 million had been deposited. He immediately transferred the entire amount to Rothstein's newly opened account.

Rothstein's wealth combined with Khalid's contacts opened doors for Scott in Casablanca and Marrakech. Scott was, Khalid reported afterward, "all business." Supposedly the plan was to invest in or develop a series of nightclubs in the country. Despite Rothstein's woes back home, Scott was, Khalid said, "in a good mood the entire time. He was always happy. He spent a lot of time at the hotel, and he loved the fact that in Morocco, he could smoke his cigars in the hotels and the restaurants whenever he wanted. He said, 'This is a nice place. I'm going to be going between the States and Morocco, back and forth.'"

Khalid's first hint something was amiss came when Rothstein decided to go home early, canceling a meeting with the mayor of Casablanca. That evening he received an apologetic call from his attorney friend at RRA, who told him that Scott had stolen millions and warned him not to return on the private charter. The next morning, Khalid drove Rothstein to the airport so as not to arise any suspicions. Before boarding the executive jet, Scott hugged Khalid, saying, "I'll see you in the States. I'll take care of you." Khalid returned by commercial airliner the following day, meeting with federal officials investigating Rothstein upon his arrival back in South Florida. Khalid gave them banking information, and, with the support of the RRA attorney, who verified his account, was able to persuade the agents that he was innocent of participation in Scott's wrongdoing. Khalid said that he did not earn a penny from his participation in the Moroccan misadventure.

Khalid and Uncle Bill were not the only company that Scott had in Morocco. Steve Caputi, Scott's longtime friend and business partner at Café Iguana, flew to North Africa, bringing along access to an account in which Scott had stashed an extra million bucks. Rothstein also flew in his loyal bodyguard, Bob Scandiffio, a fifty-year-old professional who had previously provided security for celebrities such as music executive Tommy Mottola and superstar Celine Dion. By this time, he had helped and worked with Rothstein for two years. Though he was with Scott much of the time, Scandiffio insisted he knew nothing of the Ponzi scheme—until he was summoned to Casablanca.

"I flew out to Morocco, and that's when I found out what was going on," Scandiffio said to reporter Norman. "He told me he made some bad deals, you know, but I'm not a lawyer—I didn't really know much about what he was talking about, but I kind of knew he was doing something wrong." As it turned out, Scott did not call for Scandiffio because he was lonely. Instead, he presented a plan that he hoped might benefit both men—minimizing Rothstein's time in prison and putting a small fortune in Scandiffio's pocket. Scandiffio, recently diagnosed with leukemia, believed that he had only a couple of years left to live and worried about leaving behind a young daughter. Scott's plan was that he would testify that he stole money from investors because Scandiffio threatened to kill him if he didn't. Sure, Scandiffio might die in jail, but Scott would put $250,000 into a bank account for his daughter. "He said he knew I was going to die in a couple of years because of my cancer and that they were going to take care of my child is what they were offering. I said, 'I'm going to spend the last couple of years I have with my kid to go to prison for you?'"

Scott even offered to arrange things so that he and Scandiffio could serve their time in the same prison cell. "He said, 'I have the pull to do that,'" Scandiffio remembered. "I said, 'Dude, there's no way you can do that even with the pull you got. You don't really have any pull anyway.' He kept saying, 'You're going to die anyway.'" Though Scandiffio refused Rothstein's entreaties, the two men remained friends, and he flew back on the chartered jet with Scott and Uncle Bill. "I made a promise to Scott in Morocco that I would keep my mouth shut and he would take care of me and do the right thing by me," said Scandiffio. But that proved an impossible promise to keep for both men. As soon as he got home, the FBI came calling, and Scandiffio offered up the entire story, or at least as much of it as he knew. The agents believed him, although they scoffed at Scott's plan to offload as much blame as possible onto his bodyguard's shoulders. "Did he really think that was going to work?" said Scandiffio. "Even the feds were like, 'Are you kidding me? This guy is out of his mind saying that s---.'"

Why did Scott return from a country where he was safe from extradition, where he had spirited away somewhere between $15 million and $18 million? That sum is large enough to live comfortably in Morocco even if he never earned another dollar (though not on the grand and tasteless scale of his last five years in Fort Lauderdale). Many theories have been floated. In his December 2011 bankruptcy court deposition, Rothstein indicated he had undergone a moral awakening in Morocco, saying, "I made a decision to come back, turn myself in, go to prison and tell the government everything I knew about everyone else that had committed crimes." Under questioning, he bristled at a comparison to Bernie Madoff, who received 150 years in prison for his even bigger Ponzi scheme. Madoff notoriously refused to aid federal investigators. Scott insisted that Madoff should have taken him as an example of how to do the right thing by implicating co-conspirators and helping innocent, victimized investors recuperate their money. Scott came home from the relative safety of Morocco, he insisted, "Despite the fact I knew that it was a very real possibility" that he could die in prison here.

Most Rothstein watchers in South Florida are not persuaded on this score, and I am among them. Scandiffio had a theory about Rothstein's choice: life in Morocco was not worth living, and Kim would never join Scott there, so returning was his second best option. "He said that Kim would never have went over there," said the bodyguard. "He said she wouldn't move over there and leave her family. Morocco is a filthy and dirty place. I wouldn't live over there either." When Scott asked Scandiffio what he should do, either live in exile or return to face justice, the bodyguard, like all of Rothstein's friends and advisors, counseled him to return. "I said, 'Sooner or later it's going to catch up with you.'"

Other theories include fear of being tracked down by the American mob, the Italian Mafia, or Israeli organized crime. This, I think, gets closer to the truth. Remember, Scott sought a country without extradition not only to the United States but also to Israel, which indicates he had engaged in dealings that violated Israeli law. His known association with the Levy family strengthens this idea, as does his testimony in the December 2011 depositions, when Scott mentioned laundering money for organized crime through the Ponzi scheme and his manipulation of TD Bank and Gibraltar Bank, although he could not go into more specific detail.

In my mind, there is an additional reason for Scott's return. The one admirable trait I can find consistently present in Scott Rothstein's tawdry life is his devotion to family, especially his parents, but also to his wife, Kim. Keep in mind that despite public ridicule, despite being sued by the bankruptcy trustees for more than a million dollars, Kim has not divorced Scott for more than two years after he disappeared into prison and the Witness Protection Program. She is still a young and beautiful woman. Something must account for that kind of loyalty. I believe that Scott came home because he owed very bad people large sums of money, and they threatened to kill his wife, parents, and sister if he did not return and help them get some or all of it back.

Scott returned by chartered jet to Fort Lauderdale on November 3, 2009, and touched down at Fort Lauderdale

International Airport at 1:50 p.m. Much had happened during his five-day absence. The Justice Department had mounted an investigation. Stuart Rosenfeldt, with only $117,000 in RRA's bank accounts, had hired Kendall Coffey, a former US Attorney and at that time a top Miami criminal defense lawyer, to file suit against Scott and request a Broward circuit court judge to place the firm into receivership. The judge obliged. In his pleading, Coffey blamed Rothstein for the investment fraud perpetrated under the RRA name. On the day that Rothstein's plane touched down at Fort Lauderdale Executive Airport, with Uncle Bill and Robert Scandiffio in tow, retired Miami-Dade circuit court judge Herbert Stettin was appointed bankruptcy trustee to oversee the dismantling of RRA and to work in the interests of Scott's victims.

In an attempt to salvage the reputations of the firm's other lawyers, Coffey organized a media tour of Scott's "bunker," the posh inner office that only he, Debra Villegas, Irene Stay,

IRS and FBI agents outside Scott Rothstein's Harbor Beach home. (Courtesy *South Florida Business Journal*)

and—occasionally—Stuart Rosenfeldt had security access to. Listening devices, video cameras, and a controlled-access entry system protected Rothstein's inner sanctum, along with its private elevator. Reporters and cameramen from newspapers and television stations ogled Rothstein's luxurious corner office with its wall of photos showing Scott with celebrities, athletes, and politicians. It was a highly effective publicity stunt that made Scott look paranoid, controlling, and addicted to luxury, while the other lawyers in the firm became his victims.

Many of us in the South Florida business community were surprised when Rothstein was not immediately arrested upon his arrival. Speculation then ran to the question of whether he would show up at RRA's downtown offices. Within half an hour, Fort Lauderdale police, some wearing bulletproof vests, swarmed every entrance to the Las Olas Boulevard office tower, apparently to prevent Scott from entering the building. A Fort Lauderdale police spokesman told reporters that police had been called by RRA attorneys "concerned about their safety." Added Stuart Rosenfeldt, "Better safe than sorry." Buddy Nevins, a local veteran reporter, mocked the response on his website: "Another overkill by the Fort Lauderdale cops? Do they really need a dozen or more armed cops, some with bulletproof vests, to deal with one middle-aged, portly lawyer?" In any event, Scott was nowhere to be seen. He did not show up for a hearing that afternoon in Broward circuit court, where Stettin was appointed bankruptcy trustee. Nor was Scott on hand the following day, when federal authorities, including FBI and IRS agents arrived to serve a search warrant at the RRA offices in the Bank of America building on Las Olas Boulevard. Rosenfeldt let them into Scott's private office suite, where more than seven hours later the agents carted away forty-four boxes of documents.

Veteran Fort Lauderdale attorney and Washington insider

Jim Blosser, a skeptic almost from the moment he met Rothstein a few years earlier at Jackson Steakhouse, watched from his office at the law firm Blosser & Sayfie, just across the street.

> We watched it unfold from the balcony and it was a spectacle, [a game of] cops and robbers being played out across the street. It was beyond imagination that something like this could occur on Las Olas Boulevard. How many times in your life do you see this type of law enforcement action across the street from your office with someone you know? Everybody was waiting for a limousine to pull up and then see Scott Rothstein step out to be arrested. It was totally like something out of a movie.

Scott failed to show up at any of the places or events where people hoped to get a glimpse of his public humiliation because he had returned with a plan. Federal authorities met his plane at the executive airport and he entered into negotiations at once. This appears to have been pre-arranged, possibly by Marc Nurik, the former RRA attorney who resigned specifically to represent Rothstein. In less than two weeks, by November 16, Scott had inked a deal not to fight the seizure of his assets, forfeiting twenty-two properties, his interest in more than one hundred companies, more than a dozen sports cars, an eighty-seven-foot yacht, art, furniture, and everything else he owned. News coverage listing the excesses of Rothstein's possessions—hundreds of cartoonish tailor-made suits, the infamous golden toilets, fetish wear for Kim—became a spectacle that entertained South Florida TV viewers and newspaper readers for several months. Multiple auctions were necessary to liquidate all of Scotts' ill-gotten and mostly tasteless junk, including the fleet of luxury cars and the collection of approximately 300 watches. Vilifying Scott in local chat rooms and in the comments sections of news blogs, such as Bob Norman's "Daily Pulp" at *New Times,* became a South Florida pastime that unfortunately, frequently veered into anti-Semitism. "We decided it would be more appropriate to turn over everything to the government," Marc Nurik, Rothstein's attorney, told reporters. Nurik said he negotiated the deal with prosecutors before Rothstein signed it, adding that his client was determined to help ensure the return of as much money as possible to innocent investors bilked in the $1.4 billion Ponzi scheme. As it turned out, that meant working closely not only with federal authorities, but also with Stettin and William Scherer, the attorney representing some of the wealthiest and most powerful investors to lose money.

Local observers were intensely curious as to why Scott was allowed to walk around free when his empire was the fruit of a $1.2 billion Ponzi scheme. The media dug into the story like the red meat it was, with excellent journalism by Bob Norman; Jon Burstein, Brittany Wallman, and Peter Franceschina at the *Sun Sentinel;* Kevin Gale and Paul Brinkman at the *South Florida Business Journal;* and John Pacenti with the *Daily Business Review.* Several reporters at the *Miami Herald,* including Jay Weaver and Mary Ellen Klaus, also contributed. One of them got through to Rothstein on his cell phone on Sunday, November 9, a conversation in which Scott downplayed the direness of his situation: "I'm sitting here smoking cigars with Marc [Nurik]. Rumors of my demise have been greatly exaggerated." Nurik chimed into debunk the widely believed idea that Scott was telling all to federal investigators. "All this nonsense that he is somehow hanging out with the government—he is free. I don't know where all this stuff comes from. I have him hidden . . . I have been discussing his case with the government . . . My client is at an undisclosed location of my choosing, and he is talking to no one but me. He hasn't even met with his family."

Bob Norman churned up scoops and insight and color on every aspect of the case, from the murder of Melissa Britt

Scott Rothstein showing off his watch collection. (Courtesy *Miami Herald*)

Lewis to the flight to Morocco. He found and interviewed Khalid, the guide, and a stripper who had been Kim Rothstein's roommate before she met Scott. When you work that hard, it pays off. The day following the *Herald* telephone interview, Norman was at the Capital Grille, Rothstein's old favorite hangout, to meet a source, when lo and behold, he spied Scott and Nurik sitting at a table. Taking out his Flip recorder, Norman walked over and introduced himself. Scott remembered him. (How could he not? This was the reporter who Rothstein, only two months earlier, threatened to "destroy" under a welter of lawsuits in the infamous "Jewish Avenger" phone call.) This time, Rothstein was cordial but subdued. The maître d' arrived to ask Rothstein how he was doing. "It's tough, it's tough," Scott said as Norman videoed the exchange. "I'm going to do the right thing, so, you know. Make sure when you see everybody, just tell them that I'm alive, I'm well, and I'm doing the right thing, you know. Make sure everything's going to get fixed properly. Everybody makes mistakes in life, and you've got to fix them." Norman asked how he was going to do that, and Scott replied, "I'm not going to answer any questions, Bob." Norman turned off the video camera and sat down to chat over a beer. In addition to Nurik, Joe Alu, one of Rothstein's longtime bodyguards, sat at a nearby table. In the ensuing conversation, Norman learned that Rothstein "hated" Morocco. Scott admitted he had put everyone in his life "through hell," and asserted he had returned to "set things right."

Nurik put an end to the questions, turning the conversation to the Dolphins, who were having a down year. Scott said that he had so much going on he couldn't concentrate on a football game. He made nice with Norman, asking if he had seen the Jewish Avenger cape local politician Steve Geller had made for him. "I love that, but you know what, you should have that," Rothstein said to Norman. "You can hold it for me. I want it back when I return. You can hold it for safekeeping." Rothstein meant back from jail, but it didn't need to be said. It was, in keeping with everything associated with Scott Rothstein, a bizarre yet somehow charming exchange.

Despite Nurik's denials, Rothstein cooperated with investigators and bankruptcy officers as fast and hard as he could. He provided so much information to lawyers representing investors that William Scherer, attorney for some of the biggest victims, including Razorback Holdings and Doug Von Allmen, wrote a letter to the judge at the sentencing hearing the following summer detailing Scott's value to Ponzi victims and requesting a sentence reduction. But Scott was doing more than providing financial information and ratting out the many people who, in one capacity or another, aided the Ponzi scheme. He went out and tried to run sting operations on criminal associates. In at least one case, it worked, hauling in a Miami-based international mobster, who served as a go-between for the Italian and American Mafias.

It happened like this. After meeting with federal authorities, the still-free Rothstein began working the phones. Among those he called was Roberto Settineri, a Miami Beach wine merchant whose real job was to act as an intermediary for the Sicilian Mafia clan, Santa Maria di Gesù of Palermo, and the Gambino crime family in New York, which had extensive business in South Florida. The FBI had been working with Italian authorities for years on an operation called Paisan Blues that targeted mobsters in both countries, including Settineri. The government had wiretapped Gambino family member Gaetano Napoli Sr., another target of the probe, as he intervened on Settineri's behalf in a dispute with other American mobsters. But the FBI could not quite muster enough evidence to arrest Settineri and close the circle of the longstanding investigation. Upon hearing that Rothstein knew Settineri, the FBI pushed Scott to make contact with him. Rothstein told Settineri, who he had met at the Versace Mansion in Miami Beach, that he had two boxes full of incriminating documents he needed shredded and some $10 million in Ponzi proceeds to be laundered. He offered Settineri $69,000 for the job. Settineri enlisted a couple of other Rothstein acquaintances to help him, Enrique Ros and Daniel Dromerhauser, partners at Five Star Executive Protection and Security, a Pembroke Pines firm that supplied security at the Versace Mansion. It is amazing to think that anyone would be naïve or greedy enough to work with Rothstein, given the wall-to-wall news coverage he was receiving since his return from Morocco. But the story Scott wove for the sting sounded credible. It does make sense that he'd have documents that he would want to destroy and millions of ill-gotten funds to hide.

Although Settineri and his buddies never actually shredded any documents, they did agree to do the job. Rothstein recorded his telephone conversations and meetings with the three men. At one meeting in Plantation on November 23, 2009, revealed in Ros's plea agreement, Rothstein discussed how to launder the $10 million. Present were Settineri, Ros, Dromerhauser, and an FBI informant posing as an art dealer. The plan was to buy art from the dealer at inflated prices, with $5 million going into an account controlled by Ros, and another $5 million going into another account, presumably for Rothstein's use.

With this wiretap evidence in hand, along with Rothstein as a witness and informant, American and Italian police were able to bring Paisan Blues to a conclusion. In March 2010, authorities spread out in cities across two continents, arresting Settineri, Ros, and Dromerhauser in Florida; Napoli and two of his sons in New York; and twenty alleged mobsters in Sicily and other Italian locations. All three Florida suspects eventually negotiated guilty pleas. Settineri was sentenced to four years in prison, while Dromerhauser and Ros each got ten months of house arrest.

I think many observers in South Florida did not appreciate the significance of Scott's participation in this international investigation, shrugging their shoulders and thinking, "One Mafia soldier and two security guards—big deal." But by completing the sting that resulted in Settineri's arrest, Scott was able to provide the capstone to a complex and expensive investigation that had been languishing. No wonder the feds are keen to guard Rothstein in the Witness Protection Program and to petition Judge Cohn for a sentence reduction.

Settineri was not the only person Scott tried to sting during his month of bonus freedom. Apparently, he went after friends, too. Muhammad "Moe" Sohail, owner of the upscale Ultimate Cigars shop on Federal Highway in Fort Lauderdale, received a call from Rothstein that put him on the alert. Scott, a cigar aficionado, was a close friend of Sohail's for six years. The two had held serious conversations about opening a new cigar shop on Las Olas Boulevard in the former Jackson Steakhouse location, to be named Bova Smoke. When Sohail's girlfriend, allegedly speeding, ran a stop light on Broward Boulevard on the afternoon of August 12, 2009, and wrecked Sohail's Bentley, Sohail called Rothstein. In turn, Scott called Fort Lauderdale Police Chief Frank Adderley, and both men converged at the scene. Sohail's girlfriend was not cited with a ticket. A driver in the other car received a ticket for failure to yield right of way while making a left turn, but the State Attorney dropped the charge.

The incident reveals, however, what close chums Sohail and Rothstein were at the time. By December, everything had changed, at least according to Sohail. "Scott called me, and he was laughing like nothing happened, like a psycho," Sohail told reporter Bob Norman. "He said, 'I'm staying in a roach motel.' I said, 'Scott, that's the least of your problems. Do you realize what you have done to your friends?'" If Sohail was feeling used, he had only to wait a few minutes. Scott started talking about former Broward County Commissioner Joe Eggelletion, who had recently been indicted on federal and state corruption charges. Scott reminded Sohail that Eggelletion was a regular customer at Ultimate Cigars, where he had received cigars as gifts. That the gifts came from Scott, not Sohail, went unmentioned. Scott told Sohail that Broward Sheriff's Office's Lt. David Benjamin would be visiting the store on an errand. Believing he was either being shaken down or set up for the feds, Sohail hung up on Scott. Benjamin never appeared at the store.

Who knows how many other "friends" Scott may have tried to entrap? Considering how he turned on Sohail and the way he plundered the accounts of Ted Morse's family—his best friend's family—of approximately $57 million, I would guess all of them. "Six years he was lying to me, and I don't call somebody like that a friend," Sohail told Bob Norman. "It hurts when you see how deceiving he is. He used to call me family. I went to his house; we spent holidays together. He was in my shop five times a week. Thank God we never did business together. It hurts what he did."

The Justice Department reined Scott in on December 1, 2009, when he was arrested on federal charges of racketeering, conspiracy to commit money laundering, conspiracy to commit fraud, wire fraud, and mail fraud. Obviously, the FBI had determined that, after a month, he could no more serve them as bait for mobsters or crooked officials. Already well acquainted with federal officers, Scott turned himself in. He was marched into the FBI office in North Miami at 8 a.m. in handcuffs. He pleaded not guilty in federal court to all counts. Two months later, on January 27, 2010, Rothstein changed his plea to guilty. He faced one hundred years in prison and was forty-seven years old. Despite the cooperation he gave the FBI and the bankruptcy court lawyers seeking to claw back funds for defrauded investors, judges took a dim view of Rothstein. US Magistrate Robin Rosenbaum denied bail, citing Scott's penchant for forgery and his flight risk.

When the time came for Scott's sentencing in June 2010, reporters and blog commenters expected him to receive a severely reduced sentence of thirty or even twenty years. Federal prosecutors, citing his continuing assistance, asked for forty years. Scott's lawyers thought that it was realistic to hope for thirty. But Judge Cohn brushed aside Scott's somewhat maudlin and unintentionally self-revealing mitigation letter. He brushed aside the prosecutor's recommendation. He brushed aside Scott's comment, just before sentencing: "I am truly and deeply sorry for what I have done. I don't expect your forgiveness. I don't. I am ashamed and embarrassed." Instead, Judge Cohn sternly lectured Rothstein on the deliberate and carefully planned nature of his crimes. "This Ponzi scheme was not the result of a poor business decision. Quite the contrary, it was fraud at its inception," said the judge. He was particularly incensed that Scott, an officer of the court, would forge the signature of judges on fake judgments. "These actions constituted the most egregious wrong a licensed attorney can commit," Judge Cohn said. "There can be no conduct more reviled."

Cohn sentenced Rothstein to fifty years in prison. Scott's mom, Gay, gasped audibly in the courtroom, shielding her eyes with a hand and leaning against a wall, according to news reports. Kim wiped tears away. A trim and weary Scott accepted his sentence stoically.

While Scott continued to provide information to the FBI in jail, a frenzy of legal activity began in his wake, as creditors and bilked investors sought to get their money back. Clawback suits were filed against Rothstein, Kim, David Boden, and many others, not to mention TD Bank and Gibraltar Bank. In January 2012, after months of testimony, a federal jury in

Miami needed only four hours to return a judgment against TD Bank in favor of Coquina Investments, a consortium of Texas investors that alleged that he bank "was integral to the fraud" and either knowingly participated in Scott's Ponzi scheme or neglected normal accounting procedures that would have caught it. The jury awarded Coquina a total of $67 million—$32 million in compensatory damages and $35 million in punitive damages. TD Bank faced another, bigger suit worth $200 million from Razorback Holdings, another investment group. The legal and financial outfall from Rothstein's Ponzi play will continue for years.

There has been speculation that Scott may help bring down additional organized crime figures, though no hard information has emerged as to whom or to when that might be. It is true that Scott mentioned laundering money through the Ponzi scheme during his December 2011 bankruptcy deposition. He also talked about corruption of public officials, mentioning police, judges, and other officers of the court. But he was not allowed to name names, prevented each time by a federal prosecutor sitting in on the questioning who cited investigative privilege. This means that mobsters, crooked cops, and judges on the take could not be named, because they may well yet be indicted.

By contrast, Scott was allowed to talk freely about Stuart Rosenfeldt, which suggested that Rosenfeldt is no longer under investigation and need not be anxious about being indicted at any point in the future. Corrupt officials who dallied with Rothstein—and they know who they are, even if we don't—should not relax just yet.

As of July 2012, eight people in addition to Rothstein had been indicted for crimes connected to the Ponzi scheme. It seems safe to say that many of these—Debra Villegas, for example—are not criminals by nature and most likely would never have run afoul of the law had they not come into the orbit of Scott Rothstein. Those eight were: Villegas, serving a ten-year sentence for forging legal documents and money laundering; RRA lawyer Howard Kusnick, disbarred and serving two years for conspiracy to commit wire fraud; nightclub owner Steve Caputi, five years for impersonating bank officials and reporters to deceive potential investors; RRA information technology experts Curtis Renie and William Cort, thirty-seven months on charges of conspiracy to commit wire fraud for building a counterfeit TD Bank website for Rothstein; Marybeth Feiss, an administrator at RRA, sentenced to six months after pleading guilty to one charge of violating election laws for laundering illegal campaign contributions by making them look like bonuses to RRA lawyers and other employees; William Boockvor, known as Uncle Bill, who pleaded guilty to wire fraud conspiracy, a maximum of five years for creating false bank statements, among other things; and RRA attorney Steven Lippman, who pleaded guilty to one count of conspiring to violate federal election laws.

Attorneys close to the Rothstein case say that as many as two dozen additional indictments can be expected in the years to come. Mobsters, law enforcement officers, public officials, and former RRA lawyers all have reason to worry. Scott provided another round of depositions for attorneys representing defrauded investors, who sought answers on his dealings with TD Bank, in June 2012. "His testimony fills in the blanks and ties everything together into a nice, neat package," Charles H. Lichtman, one of the bankruptcy trustee attorneys, told *Businessweek*. In the same story, Marc Nurik, Rothstein's lawyer, said that such testimony does not guarantee a sentenced reduction, though that is clearly for what Scott hopes. "Most of the precedent is in other types of crimes," he said. "Nobody to my knowledge has provided as much cooperation in an investment fraud."

Regardless of the indictments in Scott's wake, the damage

he caused in his egomaniacal five-year splurge is hard to calculate. On September 22, 2010, Robert Scandiffio, Rothstein's former bodyguard, shot himself to death at his apartment in Plantation. Before going to work for Scott, Scandiffio was "a chiseled 260 pounds" with a successful career as "a bodyguard to the stars," according to reporter Bob Norman. After surviving cancer and his association with the Rothstein scandal, he could no longer find work. He left behind a small daughter.

"I don't think he [Scandiffio] wanted to do anything but be a good bodyguard and be loyal to someone," said bankruptcy attorney Lichtman, who interviewed Scandiffio for hours. "The more I looked and the more I dug I don't believe Scandiffio benefitted from the scheme. He didn't have the lifestyle. He was just hurt very badly." Scandiffio brought the count to three of Rothstein employees who died by violence: one murdered, two by their own hands. While Scott cannot be tied to any of them, I cannot help but point out that in most offices employing 150 people, years—sometimes decades—pass without anyone falling victim to violence. In slightly more than five years, Scott's count stands at three. I find it impossible not to conclude that Rothstein's greed and egomania poisoned the atmosphere of everyone around him.

Although reporters were not allowed to attend the December 2011 depositions in Miami, lawyers reported that Rothstein was fit, considerably trimmer than during his Ponzi days. He wore some kind of facial hair—I imagine the salt-and-pepper mustache and goatee so popular among youngish men in the early twenty-first century. He wore Polo shirts and jeans, reportedly purchased for him by his lawyer, Nurik (or more likely someone in Nurik's office) at Target. The transcripts revealed a man who is well treated—he mentioned having access to a computer and a flat-screen TV—well-adjusted, and confident. More than once, he sparred with lawyers when he thought they were being rude or dense. He was quick to assert moral high ground, declaring his superiority to Bernie Madoff, who did not cooperate with federal authorities or bankruptcy trustees; correct lawyers who got minor facts or procedural matters wrong; and show his teeth to a lawyer who suggested he conspired to murder Melissa Britt Lewis. He named or was willing to name dozens of people who made his Ponzi scheme possible in a bid to reduce his sentence and obtain freedom at some point in his natural lifetime.

"All Ponzi schemes do the same thing," Scott said in the deposition, as though lecturing a seminar on white-collar crime. "They explode at the end." This, of course, is more than just the voice of experience. Everyone knows that Ponzi schemes collapse sooner or later; it is the nature of the con. Scott surely knew how things would end for him before he lured the first investor. So why did he do it? What onlookers are left wondering is whether it was worth the carnage, the time in prison, just for the rock-star lifestyle for barely five years.

Over the course of the years spent writing this book, I have come to the conclusion that Scott Rothstein is a criminal sociopath with an unusual combination of skill, intelligence, and surprising character traits. I think that he had an endgame in mind from the outset, one with multiple avenues of escape. One was fleeing the country, which he tried and found, for one reason or another, not to his liking. But I think Scott had another, more complex, exit strategy in place, too. I think he purposely drew as many co-conspirators as possible into his web of complicity for the express purpose of testifying against them should his other escapes fail and he wind up with a long prison sentence. What we are now witnessing is Scott's long con, turning evidence against friends, family members, employees, and co-workers—anyone whose prosecution might induce Judge Cohn to reduce Scott's prison sentence and let him out of jail. Though behind bars, cosseted in the Witness Protection Program, Scott Rothstein remains as devious and manipulative as ever. I would not bet against him.

Epilogue

Summer 2012 in South Florida became steamy with additional developments in the Scott Rothstein fraud that featured mega-litigation during the first five months of the year. In addition to more than fifty pending civil cases and long-awaited indictments with co-conspirators, hedge funds from Texas to New York continued to battle against Canada's second-largest bank, TD Bank.

Coquina Investments, a Texas-based investment group, produced emails in June 2012, proving there were "lock letters" on bank stationary that convinced Rothstein's investors that their money was secure and in the bank.

"The significance of this new evidence is hard to overstate," wrote attorney David Mandel, representing Coquina, which last had won a $67 million jury verdict in January.

The TD Bank emails surfaced from a pending civil case by Emess Capital of New York, which is scheduled for late 2012. It has become clear that attorneys representing Rothstein investor victims are focused on the deep pockets of TD Bank, which during the past decade have enjoyed tremendous success with expansion on the eastern seaboard, resulting in a status of the sixth-largest banking institution in the United States. The civil case by Coquina against TD has caught the attention of other banks.

"It is a landmark case that will cause banks around the world to shudder," Charles Intriago, president of the Association of Certified Financial Crime Specialists, told

The Economist magazine. "The cases against TD are helping victims of fraud everywhere to compile a road map on how to recover their losses from deep-pocketed financial institutions."

During the first week of May 2012, a $10 million settlement was reached with Rothstein's former accounting firm, Berenfeld Spritzer Shechter & Sheer of Coral Gables. The accountants became Rothstein's pals in the same way that the bankers did, enjoying a lifestyle full of major sporting events and the pleasures of twenty-something-years-old women. This philandering, of course, has led to the end of many professional careers.

Another of Rothstein's banks, Gibraltar Private Bank & Trust, with $1.6 billion in assets, dismissed CEO Steven Hayworth in May. His departure came after the bank reached a $10 million settlement in February with investors.

The ninth person to plead guilty in the case was Steven Lippman, who admitted to conspiring to violate federal election laws and to commit bank fraud. His sentencing has yet to be concluded and he faces up to five years in prison. Lippman's crimes include making large contributions to Senator John McCain's 2008 presidential campaign and then receiving illegal reimbursement from Rothstein.

Next to be indicted that May were George Levin and Frank Preve, believed to be two of the biggest feeders of the Ponzi scheme. The Securities and Exchange Commission charged the two men with a total of six counts of violations after they raised more than $157 million from 173 investors. The issuing of promissory notes from Levin's company took place over a period of two years. Then, they used the investor funds to purchase Rothstein's fake legal settlements.

According to the SEC, Levin and Preve sought new investor money while "falsely touting the continued success of their investment strategy." With their fate tied to that of Rothstein, Levin and Preve's settlement-purchasing business collapsed along with the Ponzi scheme.

"Levin and Preve fueled Rothstein's Ponzi scheme with the false sense of security they gave investors," said Eric I. Bustillo, a regional director of the SEC. "They promised to safeguard investors' assets, but gave Rothstein money with nothing to show for it."

Preve wrote in a July 2008 email, "Missing documents . . . these won't go away so someone needs to do them . . . you are also holding up our audit because I can't show anyone that I am a complete idiot by sending out millions of dollars with nothing to show for it except some emails that say 'Hey, Guido, send me 5 Mill . . . I have such a deal for you.'"

The SEC provided this email as an example that Preve knew that what he was doing wasn't proper. These two guys could face a lot more trouble in the near future. The dozens of investigations have many more indictments on the horizon, and it wouldn't surprise me to see more serious charges against these two men.

Rothstein began his second round of depositions during the first week of June 2012, as his audience of attorneys gathered at the US Attorney's Office in Fort Lauderdale. The purpose of the three-week-long deposition is to allow attorneys the opportunity to ask questions about such things as emails and other investigations relating to pending trials. Most of the transcripts are comprised of standard questions and answers; however, there are new claims against specific individuals, including former RRA attorneys Grant Smith and Christina Kitterman.

One of Rothstein's first claims was that Smith, who was promoted to the firm's management team during the final year of the Ponzi scheme, knew about illegal campaign finance activities. Smith responded to an interview request by the *South Florida Business Journal* with the following statement: "During my time at the firm, I did not participate, help, or have knowledge of any of Rothstein's crimes including any violation of campaign finance laws."

Rothstein's former law student at Nova Southeastern University, Kitterman is claimed to have impersonated an official of the Florida Bar during conversations with an investor. In his testimony, Rothstein claimed that "Kitterman was the person who played Adrian Quintella, the Florida Bar rep."

I personally know Smith and Kitterman through charitable organizations, and in response to Rothstein's allegations I believe that he is attempting only to throw more former employees under the bus. Although they both have declined my invitations to be interviewed, it seems to me that they would not commit an illegal act of that caliber that would jeopardize their careers. Rothstein's motivations of trying to receive a reduced sentence when he returns before Judge Cohn are evident after singing like a canary.

After 950 pages of the transcripts were released, Rothstein's most interesting claims include those of a police officer committing "various illegal acts," more ties with organized crime, and an 8.91-carat diamond of which he does not remember the whereabouts. Might he have forgotten Kim No. 2? Perhaps this is the reason why, as of this summer, Kim Rothstein is believed to still be married to Scott more than two years after the crime, the girlfriends, and the sex sprees were uncovered.

Scott also claimed during the deposition that he had sent a police officer to the offices of Silversea Cruises to keep an executive there from detecting a major embezzlement. Rothstein did not name the officer or agency, although speculators guess that the cop could be one of his close Broward Sheriff's Office buddies.

Rothstein stated that his friend Albert Peter, the former CEO of Silversea Cruises, feared that Chairman Manfredi Lefebvre d'Ovidio would fly in from Europe and uncover his embezzlement. So the ultimate Ponzi schemer devised a plan in which the CEO would be falsely investigated for his involvement in a prostitution sting—Rothstein sent the officer to visit the corporate offices to seek out Lefebvre, instead of allowing Lefebvre to seek out Rothstein's embezzlement.

"We had the police officer telling people that he had to find Mr. Lefebvre and that he was not going to stop until he was able to get a hold of him," stated Rothstein.

Rothstein testified to being hired to provide law firm services for Silversea Cruises through his friend Stanley Coniglio. Scott added that he knew Coniglio to "be associated with an organized crime family."

Coniglio, born in 1942, told the *Sun Sentinel* that he has never been involved with organized crime. I do believe that Rothstein had involvement with low-level mobsters, but I attribute his return from Morocco to his lack of common sense in ripping off more prominent organized crime figures. Time will tell as to whether Coniglio is one of those people.

One of the anticipated questions that went unanswered at the June deposition was the location of Rothestein's 12.08-carat diamond ring. The answer was revealed on Wednesday, September 6, when Kim Rothstein and two friends were charged with hiding more than $1 million in jewelry from federal investigators and the bankruptcy court. The loot contained the "intense yellow" diamond ring, luxury watches, various jewelry, coins, and fifty one-ounce gold bars. Federal investigators charged Kim; her attorney, Scott Saidel; and her friend Stacie Weisman with single counts of conspiracy to commit money laundering. Each faces five years in federal prison. The charges were filed in "criminal information," however, that kind of legal prosecution often indicates that a plea agreement for something less than the maximum penalty has already been reached.

Related charges were filed against a man named Eddy Marin, who allegedly acted a fence for Kim, and Patrick

Daoud, president of Fort Lauderdale's Daoud Jewelers. Both are accused of perjury and obstruction, which carry a possible twenty-year sentence.

Earlier, during the clawback process, when federal bankruptcy lawyers sought to recover money and property that could be used to pay Scott's Ponzi scheme victims, Kim had testified under oath that she had turned over all assets, including jewelry.

Kim's arrogant protestations of innocence go back to 2009, when Scott's Ponzi scheme came crashing down. In November 2009, my suspicions were aroused when a friend called to tell me that Kim was in a jewelry store on Seventeenth Causeway. I drove to the store, where my friend and I saw Kim and bodyguard Joe Alu standing at the counter with twelve men's watches arrayed in front of them. Kim was having them resized so that they could be worn or sold as women's watches.

Turning from the counter, Kim and Alu came face to face with my friend and me. I reintroduced myself as the writer who had left phone messages requesting an interview. She was not pleased to see me. "I can't go anywhere these days," she snapped. "I can't even get batteries for my watches." After a pause, she added, "It's not like I'm unloading my watches or anything like that."

Kim was actually telling the truth, although she could not have looked or sounded guiltier than she did that day. The unloading of watches and other jewelry came months later, according to the September 2012 indictment.

Apparently, federal investigators were determined to find the missing property and to nail Kim for concealing it. "When a witness lies under oath, the integrity of our system is undermined, and he or she will be held accountable," US Attorney Wilfredo Ferrer said.

Through her new attorneys, David Tucker and David

Kotler, Kim issued a statement of contrition, taking "full responsibility for her actions" in hiding assets. "Kim would like to take the opportunity to express her disappointment, shame, and sadness in regard to all of the victims of her husband, Scott Rothstein's actions related to the Ponzi scheme for which he has previously been sentenced," wrote Tucker and Kotler in a statement. "She had no involvement or knowledge of his fraudulent activity.

The statement from Kim's lawyers refers to Scott as her "husband," which leaves the impression that they were still married as of September 2012, almost three years after the collapse of the Rothstein empire on Halloween 2009. I'm sure that I'm not alone in finding it curious that an attractive woman approaching early middle-age would remain married to a notorious criminal who is set to remain in prison for the next half-century.

Or will he? Based on my research and on Scott's performance in the most recent rounds of bankruptcy court depositions, I believe that he most likely ratted Kim out on the hidden jewelry and assets. He has made no secret of his fervent desire to shorten his prison sentence—and his willingness to betray anyone to get it.

Moving forward, we certainly will hear of more developments in the Rothstein case, which most likely will include additional stories of mobsters, escorts, and perhaps even elected officials. After interviewing dozens of people, who in one way or another were connected to Rothstein, the one person who I feel was the most fortunate to have escaped unscathed is Ms. Lauderdale, the young lady who was almost engaged to Scott prior to his marriage to Kim.

A recent college graduate at the time of meeting Rothstein, Ms. Lauderdale admitted she was young and naive when her relationship began with Rothstein. I continue to refer to her as Ms. Lauderdale because of her professional status today in the Broward County community. Fortunately, she still has a lifetime ahead of sun in the paradise of Fort Lauderdale, which had almost brought her to disaster.

"I was removed, but holy s---, I could've been Kim," Ms. Lauderdale told me.

> After it happened [the collapse], my father called. He said "I'm reading about a Scott Rothstein from Fort Lauderdale who did a billion dollar Ponzi scheme." I'm cringing on the phone and he said, "Please don't tell me that this is the Scott Rothstein who you dated for a while."
>
> I said, "Yes, yes it is." My father and I are very close. I remember him pausing. His silence was like daggers to my chest. I thought, "Oh my God, here it comes." And he said, "You're one lucky girl. I remember the day when you called and said 'I don't know what's going on but I like this guy and he is older. He's going to move quickly soon with our relationship.'" I do feel fortunate.

I only hope there will be similar relief for the remaining survivors of Scott Rothstein's devastating tornado. The biggest motivation for spending more than two years writing this book is to document the lessons learned from his rise and fall, so that the precedent of committed crimes will be more easily recognized. Hardest hit were the shoulders of charitable organizations, the people who help our community to better itself. Hopefully, in the future, men such as Scott Rothstein as documented here can be stopped before causing any extraordinary damage. For now, it is best remembered that if a wealthy philanthropist arrives in a town overnight, it is a good idea to determine from where his—or her—money comes before accepting any donations or any terms of employment. Scott Rothstein set out to make his mark on the Fort Lauderdale community, and for better or for worse, that is exactly what he did. Now, it is up to us to pick up his tangled pieces.